Remarkable
Muslim Women
Throughout the Ages

REMARKABLE Muslim Women
Throughout the Ages
20 Stories of Faith, Courage & Resilience

Approved by Shaykh Dr Saalim Al-Azhari

Maryam Yousaf

Remarkable Muslim Women Throughout the Ages
20 Stories of Faith, Courage & Resilience

First published in 2022 by Muslima Today
Email: askmuslimatoday@gmail.com
Website: www.muslimatoday.com

Text and Illustrations Copyright © Maryam Yousaf, 2022
All rights reserved.

The right of Maryam Yousaf to be identified as the author of this work has been asserted by her in accordance with the Copyright, Designs and Patents Act, 1988.

No part of this publication may be reproduced, stored or transmitted in any form or by any means, electronic, mechanical, photocopying, recording or otherwise, without prior permission of the publisher.

First Edition
Verified by: Shaykh Dr Saalim Al-Azhari
Edited by: Laura El Alam, Jessica Hassan, and Zainab bint Younus
Cover and Interior Design by: Sheeba Shaikh

ISBN: 978-0-9934078-8-8 paperback

To the four greatest women in history
– Aasiya bint Muzahim, Maryam bint Imran,
Khadijah bint Khuwaylid and Fatima bint Muhammad ﷺ.

To my beloved family, and to my Ummi Sultana,
my Nani Fatima, my Nani-Maa Amira. May Allah grant you
Jannat-ul-Firdous.

To the light of my eyes;
Hana, Jannah, Dawud, and Danyaal.

To my remarkable readers and to all the remarkable
women who haven't been included in this book but are all
worthy of being mentioned.

Contents

Introduction	8
Haajar (Pre-Islamic Arabia)	13
Aasiya bint Muzahim (Egypt)	19
Khadijah bint Khuwaylid (6th century, Pre-Islamic Arabia)	27
Aisha bint Abu Bakr (7th century, Arabia)	39
Rufaida al-Aslamiyyah (7th century, Arabia)	47
Nusayba bint Ka'ab (7th century, Arabia)	53
Fatima al-Fihri (9th century, Ifriqiyyah)	65
Raziya Sultan (13th century, Delhi Sultanate)	73
Sayyida al-Hurra (15th century, al-Andalus)	81
Nana Asma'u (19th century, Sokoto Caliphate)	89
Cut Nyak Dhien (19th century, Aceh Sultanate, Sumatra Island)	97
Lady Evelyn Cobbold (19th century, Scotland)	103
Şule Yüksel Şenler (20th century, Turkey)	111
Zainab al-Ghazali (20th century, Egypt)	119
Rebiya Kadeer (20th century, East Turkestan)	127

Hawa Aden Mohamed (20th century, Somalia)   137

Anisa Rasooli (20th century, Afghanistan)   145

Sara Minkara (20th century, United States)   151

Arfa Karim (20th century, Pakistan)   157

Razan al-Najjar (20th century, Palestine)   163

Acknowledgements   169

Glossary   170

Bibliography   177

About the Author   184

Introduction

In the name of Allah ﷺ, the Most Gracious, the Most Merciful

Welcome to *Remarkable Muslim Women Throughout the Ages*, a book that tells the stories of twenty amazing Muslim women from the past and present. Today, Muslim women who do something inspirational or extraordinary are often asked if they are breaking a stereotype. My answer to that is 'no'. Muslim women have been at the forefront of society from the very beginning of human existence, and especially since the last and final Messenger Muhammad ﷺ came with the final revelation of Allah. They have been making positive contributions both at home – nurturing and raising a great nation – and in wider society contributing to the advancement of education and making the world a better place. Despite this, their achievements are often little known. However, Allah ﷻ knows, and in the end that is what truly matters.

> *As for those who believe and do good deeds. We do not let the reward of anyone who does a good deed go to waste.* Qur'an, Surah al-Kahf, 18:30

I wrote this book as a celebration of the lives of these phenomenal Muslim women who are real-life heroes who are better than any fictional characters. Muslim women have had a powerful presence in many spheres over the centuries. They have been scholars, writers, entrepreneurs, teachers, warriors, activists, founders, mothers, wives, poets, sovereigns, elected leaders, judges, computer scientists and more. We can empower the women and the generations of the future by celebrating the legendary Muslim women of the past and present.

In this day and age, Muslim girls like you are bombarded by social media celebrities and influencers. It is often confusing to look up to someone as a role model and then to be disappointed by their actions. We all need positive role models: people who are examples of exemplary faith and character to look up to. We may be inspired by their modest fashion or their positive Muslim lifestyle. However, the truth is that we are all human, and our faith can fluctuate. Unfortunately, people in the public eye sometimes begin as a good example to the thousands of girls who look up to them, only to later abandon their principles after acquiring vast fame and fortune. Sadly, this leaves many impressionable Muslim girls heartbroken, confused and feeling betrayed by the very people they helped elevate to celebrity status. It can even impact their faith practice negatively.

We need role models who don't abandon us based on impulse or worldly desires. Trustworthy role models can be found from Islamic history, such as the Mothers of the Believers, the women who were promised Paradise, and the Sahaabiyaat (female companions of the Prophet Muhammad ﷺ). These women were sincere and steadfast in their faith and surrendered themselves to Allah. These women displayed firmness of faith and principle. As a result, they became the epitome of righteous believers.

Muslim girls must see themselves reflected in the books they read so they can be inspired to reach their true potential and see their true worth. In the words of one of the most important scholars in Islam; women are half the Ummah and they give birth to the other half, *so they are the whole Ummah* (Ibn Al Qayyim). This is why a book like this is so important – to highlight the amazing stories of truly amazing role models for Muslim girls and women. We can, God willing, learn valuable lessons from their lives. The Messenger of Allah ﷺ said, 'The word of wisdom is the lost property of the believer. Wherever he finds it, he is most deserving of it' (*Sunan al-Tirmidhi*, no. 2687).

In selecting the twenty women for this book, I have included a diverse selection, highlighting Muslims of different races, ethnicities, nationalities and backgrounds. No one is superior to anyone else because of anything but their piety. On the topic of racism, Islam is clear. As Prophet Muhammad ﷺ said in his last sermon: 'All humankind is from Adam and Eve. An Arab has no superiority over a non-Arab nor does a non-Arab have any superiority over an Arab. A person with white skin has no superiority over a person with black skin nor does a person with black skin have any superiority over a person with white skin except by piety and good deeds' (*Musnad Ahmad*, no. 22978). We are all one because we are the children of Adam, the servants of Allah and a single ummah that should stand united. We should celebrate our diversity and not allow it to divide us.

Allah ﷺ tells us in the Qur'an:

> *O people! We created you from a male and a female, and made you races and tribes, that you may know one another. The best among you in the sight of God is the most*

righteous. God is All-Knowing, Well-Experienced. Qur'an, Surah al-Hujurat, 49:13

When writing this book, I found a common theme: nearly all the women whom I've written about had a supportive father, brother or husband. This highlights the importance of men who appreciate and support their daughters, wives, and sisters in their pursuit of excellence. There is a saying, 'Behind every great man is a great woman,' and it appears that often, the inverse is also true. Of course, all goodness is ultimately from Allah ﷻ.

I am sure you will be just as inspired as I am by the resilience, struggles, and sacrifice of the women in this book: women who were fuelled by their faith and their thirst for justice.

I have included reflections at the end of each story in the hope that we can all, God willing, benefit from the lessons in them and apply them to our daily lives. Across the world, women are widely admired for their beauty, but their stories and lives are more meaningful than their physical appearances. In the end, it is the beauty of the heart and actions that are our true legacies.

I pray that Allah ﷻ will help you and I to reach our full potential. I ask that He enables us, like the legendary women in this book, to stand up for justice and Islam, to serve others, to do good in the world and to leave a blessed legacy behind. Ameen. No matter what corner of the world we come from or what age or time we live in, we are connected by the deep roots of our faith and are all remarkable in our unique way. Please remember Allah ﷻ is the one who gives us value. The ultimate success in life is the purity of our hearts.

The Day when there will not benefit (anyone) wealth or children. But only one who comes to Allah ﷻ with a sound heart. Qur'an, Surah al-Shu'ara, 26:89

Maryam Yousaf

Disclaimer: I am not a historian or a scholar. However, a sincere effort has been made to ensure the accuracy of the information provided in this book. Shaykh Dr Saalim Al-Azhari, who is a graduate of the prestigious Al-Azhar University, has verified and approved the factual information in this book.

Parental guidance is advised. Some stories contain material that parents may find unsuitable for younger children, including a mention of FGM (female genital mutilation) in the story of Hawa Aden.

Note to the reader:
❉ This symbol appears after the name of Allah. It says 'jalla jalaaluhu,' which means 'may His glory be exalted.'

❉ This symbol appears after the name of the Prophet Muhammad ❉. It says 'sallalahu 'alayhi wa sallam,' which means 'may the peace and blessings of Allah be upon him.'

❉ This symbol appears after the name of prophets, Jibreel ❉, Haajar ❉, and Aasiya ❉. It says 'alayhis salam' which means 'peace be upon him/her.'

❉ This symbol appears after the names of the male companions of the Prophet ❉. It says 'radiallahu 'anhu' which means 'may Allah be pleased with him'.

❉ This symbol appears after the names of the wives and female companions of the Prophet ❉. It says 'radiallahu 'anha' which means 'may Allah be pleased with her'.

It is encouraged to say the appropriate salutations after these names. In the absence of a symbol, I trust readers will say the salutations whenever a blessed name is mentioned.

Haajar

A Woman of Exemplary Faith and Devotion to Allah ﷻ
Pre-Islamic Arabia

Haajar ﵂ was the second wife of Prophet Ibrahim ﵇. Sarah ﵂, the first wife of Ibrahim, had longed for a child but was unable to conceive, and she had now reached old age. She asked Prophet Ibrahim ﵇ to marry Haajar ﵂, a gift given to her by a tyrant king. Her hope was that Haajar ﵂ would bear him a child who would be his successor in prophethood. Praise be to Allah ﷻ, Haajar ﵂ and Prophet Ibrahim ﵇ married and were soon blessed with a son called Ismail, who would become a prophet of Allah ﷻ like his father. Many years later, despite her old age, Sarah ﵂ would also give birth to a son, Is'haaq, who would also become a prophet.

Allah ﷻ commanded Prophet Ibrahim ﵇ to take Haajar ﵂ and Ismail from Palestine to Makkah and to leave his beloved wife and baby in a deserted valley where there was nothing and no one to be seen. The only food they had was some dates and water in a waterskin. As he was leaving, Haajar said 'O Ibrahim! Where are you going, leaving us in this valley where there is no person whose company we may enjoy, nor is there anything (to enjoy)?' She repeated this many times, but he did not look back at her. Then she asked him: 'Has Allah commanded you to do so?' He said: 'Yes.' She said: 'Then He will not neglect us.' *(Sahih al-Bukhari*, no. 3365). Haajar ﷺ was a firm believer in Allah ﷻ, and despite the difficult and worrisome situation she was placed in, she trusted her Creator's plan. The separation was heart-wrenching, yet both husband and wife submitted to Allah's ﷻ command. Ibrahim ﷺ prayed for his wife and son's protection:

> *Our Lord! I have settled some of my offspring in a barren valley, near Your Sacred House, our Lord, so that they may establish prayer. So make the hearts of people incline towards them and provide them with fruits, so perhaps they will be thankful.*
> Qur'an, Surah Ibrahim, 14:37

When Haajar's ﷺ milk dried up, her baby cried incessantly due to thirst and hunger. Desperately in need of provisions and water for her thirsty baby, Haajar ﷺ searched for water, running back and forth between the two mountains known as Safa and Marwa seven times. She climbed to the top of Safa and then rushed to the top of Marwa, praying to Allah ﷻ for aid. Finally, both her prayers and that of Ibrahim were answered!

Allah ﷻ sent Angel Jibreel ﷺ to strike the earth with his heels – and a beautiful, clear spring of water miraculously gushed forth. The flow of water was so strong and powerful that Haajar ﷺ cried out, "Zam, zam!" ("Stop, stop!") and dug the earth around it into a basin to collect the water. She scooped the water into her waterskin and drank until she was finally able to

suckle Ismail and quench his thirst.

The Messenger of Allah ﷺ said, 'May Allah bestow mercy on Ismail's mother! Had she let the Zamzam [flow without trying to control it], Zamzam would have been a river flowing across the surface of the earth.'

The angel said to her, 'Do not be afraid of being neglected, for this is the site on which the House of Allah ﷻ will be built by this boy and his father, and Allah ﷻ will never neglect His people' (*Sahih al-Bukhari*, no. 3364).

The sacred water known as Zamzam flows to this day and is a blessing and source of nourishment for millions of pilgrims every year.

Haajar's running from one hilltop to the other seven times – known as sa'ee – is one of the rituals of the blessed pilgrimage to Makkah (Hajj and Umrah), which every Muslim, male or female, must perform. Haajar ؑ was an exemplary woman with remarkable patience and unshakeable faith. She was a devoted servant of Allah ﷻ, a loyal wife of the Prophet Ibrahim ؑ, and a loving mother to Prophet Ismail ؑ.

Later in life, Prophet Ibrahim ؑ and Prophet Ismail ؑ built the Ka'bah. Whilst they were raising the foundations of the Ka'bah, Prophet Ibrahim ؑ made the following dua:

> *Our Lord and send among them a messenger from themselves who will recite to them Your verses and teach them the Book and wisdom and purify them. Indeed, You are the Exalted in Might, the Wise.* Qur'an, Surah al-Baqarah, 2:129

Allah ﷻ ultimately answered Prophet Ibrahim's ﷺ supplication by sending the final Messenger Muhammad ﷺ and revealing the Qur'an to him.

Reflections

- Both Haajar ﷺ and Sarah ﷺ were tested, and they were compensated with blessed offspring (prophets) and the greatest nations in history. The blessed family of Prophet Ibrahim ﷺ is mentioned in our five obligatory prayers and is revered by all monotheistic faiths.

- Haajar ﷺ is important in Islam as an example of someone with unwavering faith. She did not doubt Allah's ﷻ commands or her husband's actions. She knew with certainty that Allah ﷻ would protect her and her child.

- Her desperate struggle to find water for her baby was real. She didn't sit in one spot but took the initiative and ran from one mountain to another until Allah ﷻ granted them a miracle with the most blessed water in the world today – Zamzam.

- Zamzam water has many blessings. It is mentioned in a hadith that 'the water of Zamzam is for whatever purpose it is drunk for' (*Sunan Ibn Majah*, no. 3062). This means that, God willing, Zamzam water fulfils the supplication of the one who drinks it. The next time you drink Zamzam, make a personal dua and be grateful for the blessings of Allah ﷻ!

- During her emotional and physical struggles, Haajar ﷺ remained steadfast, and in return, Allah ﷻ made her actions an act of worship. Hajj and Umrah are not complete without running between Safa and

Marwa (the two mountains), re-enacting her actions.

- Haajar is an unforgettable woman in Islam whose memory lives on in the hearts and actions of every pilgrim. She is from one of the most blessed families ever to grace the earth. Muslims supplicate for the family of Ibrahim in every prayer, in the *du'a of durood/Salawaat Ibrahimiyyah*.

- When things are not going our way, we should pray to Allah ﷻ and trust that His plans are better than our own. We may not see the wisdom behind the hardship we face straightaway, but many people look back after a hardship has passed and are grateful to Allah ﷻ for the lessons and hidden blessings in it.

Discussion Questions
1. How do you think Haajar ؑ felt at first when she and her baby were left in the barren desert without any explanation?
2. When Allah ﷻ commands us to do a certain act of worship that we have no understanding of, why is it important that we do it whether we understand the reason for it or not? What do we learn from Haajar's ؑ story about this?
3. How many times did Haajar ؑ run between Safa and Marwa?
4. What did the Muslim Ummah gain through the actions of Haajar ؑ? What were those actions, and what do we have because of them?

Aasiya bint Muzahim

*A Righteous Queen, the Guardian of Musa ﷺ,
and a Woman of Perfect Faith*
Egypt

Aasiya bint Muzahim ﷺ came from an affluent family in ancient Egypt, and her father was an important man. Unfortunately, her marriage was arranged with Pharaoh – a vicious tyrant. Pharaoh believed himself to be God and forced everyone to worship him. If they didn't, he would torture them to death. Pharaoh oppressed and enslaved the Children of Israel, the direct descendants of Prophet Yaqub ﷺ. Despite being married to the most evil of men, Aasiya ﷺ remained generous and compassionate. She was a benevolent queen who had all the riches of the world, and a heart of gold. However, despite her wealth and status, she was unable to have children of her own, which caused her great sorrow.

One night, Pharoah had a disturbing dream, he saw a fire burning the people of Egypt and their homes, but the fire did not harm the Children of Israel. When he enquired about its meaning, he was told there would be a boy born among these people who will destroy his kingdom and the people of Egypt.

This news outraged Pharaoh. He was terrified, and to ensure that the dream would never come true, he ordered that any male child born from the Children of Israel be killed. However, his ministers warned him that this would be bad for their slave labour, therefore instead he instituted a policy of killing the baby boys one year and letting them live for another.

Musa ﷺ, who was from the Children of Israel, was in great danger as soon as he was born. Allah ﷻ inspired Musa's mother to place him into the Nile River. Although it was emotionally devastating, Musa's mother had no choice but to take drastic action to save her child's life. She placed her complete trust in Allah ﷻ and was certain that her baby would be protected.

Allah ﷻ fulfilled His promise to protect Musa ﷺ. He commanded the waves to be calm and gentle as they carried the basket containing the future prophet. Under the instruction of her mother, Musa's sister followed the floating basket along the riverbank. Peeking through the reeds that covered the riverbank, she watched as the palace servants discovered the basket with baby Musa inside it. When they revealed their surprising find to Pharoah and Aasiya ﷺ, Aasiya ﷺ immediately fell in love with the beautiful baby boy who blinked up at her. Aasiya ﷺ begged Pharoah to let her keep the baby and raise him as their own son. Little did they know that this tiny baby was destined to become a prophet of Allah ﷻ.

Allah tells us in the Qur'an:

> *Pharaoh's wife said to him, 'This baby is a source of joy for me and*

Aasiya bint Muzahim

you. Do not kill him. Perhaps he may be useful to us or we may adopt him as a son.' They were unaware of what was to come.
Qur'an, Surah al-Qasas, 28:9

Pharaoh, who loved Aasiya ﷺ, reluctantly agreed to let her keep baby Musa. Who would have imagined that the very child who posed the greatest threat to Pharaoh's tyranny would grow up in his own palace, right under his nose?

Aasiya ﷺ accepted Musa ﷺ as her own child and gave him the love, comfort and security of a devoted mother. The first problem she came across was feeding the baby! Although she brought in many wet nurses to provide him with milk, he refused to feed from any of them. When this news reached Musa's sister, she told the people of the palace that she knew a woman whom no baby had rejected. The people of the palace were delighted but did not know that this was Musa's birth mother. At last, Musa was in the arms of his mother who missed him deeply. Musa happily suckled her milk until his hunger was relieved. Thus, Allah ﷻ allowed Musa's mother to be secretly close to her child once again.

After many significant events, Musa ﷺ discovered that he was a special Prophet whom Allah ﷻ chose and spoke to directly. He was commanded to teach the people to worship none but Allah ﷻ. Pharaoh was furious at Musa ﷺ, whose message challenged Pharoah's demands that the people worship him as a god.

Aasiya ﷺ, however, believed Musa's ﷺ message as soon as

it reached her ears. She knew how evil and heartless Pharaoh was, and that he was only a human being and not God, as he claimed. Despite understanding that her life would be endangered if Pharaoh ever discovered her belief in Allah ﷻ, she continued to secretly worship Him.

Pharaoh had other wives with whom he had children. One day, whilst a hairdresser was combing the hair of Pharaoh's daughter, the comb that she was using fell from her hand and the hairdresser exclaimed, 'Bismillah (in the name of Allah ﷻ)!' Pharaoh's daughter glanced at the hairdresser in confusion and asked, 'Don't you mean "in the name of my father"?' The hairdresser corrected her. 'No! My Lord and the Lord of your father is Allah ﷻ.'

Pharaoh's daughter immediately rushed to her father to tell him about the hairdresser's words. Pharaoh was outraged and had no mercy. He cruelly ordered that the hairdresser and her children be thrown, one by one, into a large container of boiling oil. She was forced to watch her children tortured and murdered by Pharaoh. As unbearable as it was, she remained strong. When her last child was brought forth – an infant so young that he was still breastfeeding – her heart faltered with grief. In that moment, Allah caused a miracle to happen: the baby opened his mouth and spoke clearly to his mother. 'Throw me into the fire! The torture and the punishment of this world are light compared to the ones in the Hereafter.' This miracle filled the hairdresser's heart with courage, even as her infant was seized from her and thrown into the oil. Before Pharoah's soldiers pushed her into the boiling pot, she showed no fear and had only one request: that her children's bones be gathered in one cloth and buried with hers.

When Aasiya ﷺ witnessed the hairdresser's courage, her own faith was strengthened. Aasiya ﷺ stood up to her husband, declaring that she disbelieved in him. She bravely told him that she believed in the Lord of Musa, the Lord of Harun (the brother of Musa ﷺ, who was also a prophet) and the Lord of the worlds – Allah ﷻ.

In his rage, Pharaoh dragged Aasiya ﷺ – a woman who had lived as a pampered queen her entire life – to the desert and tied her down. He starved her of food and water. He tormented her repeatedly, exposing her to the blazing sun, but Allah ﷻ sent down angels from the heavens to shade her with their wings. Physically broken by the torture, Aasiya's ﷺ faith was unshaken: she gazed up to the heavens and called upon Allah:

> *Oh Allah ﷻ build for me, with You, a home in Jannah!* Qur'an, Surah al-Tahrim, 66:11

Glory be to Allah ﷻ! Allah ﷻ opened up the skies for Aasiya ﷺ, so that she could look upon her palace in Jannah. Shaded by the angels and witnessing the beauty that Allah ﷻ had revealed to her, Aasiya ﷺ was overcome with joy. Infuriated by her reaction, Pharoah ordered his guards to bring forth the biggest boulder they could find and to crush her body with it if she persisted in her belief in Allah ﷻ. However, Allah ﷻ took her soul before the boulder reached her lifeless body and gave her the palace in Jannah she had so deeply longed for.

Aasiya bint Muzahim ﷺ was an extraordinary woman of perfect faith and immense courage. She is one of the four women who perfected their faith and are promised Jannah. Despite being brutally persecuted, she never wavered in her firm belief. Pharaoh was a strong and powerful ruler, but Allah ﷻ is All Powerful and gives victory to the believers in the end.

Reflections

- Aasiya ﷺ sacrificed the palace she had in this world for a palace in Jannah and to be next to Allah ﷻ. She chose to bear the suffering of this world so that she could have ease in the hereafter. She understood that this world and all its pleasures and pains are only temporary. Jannah, however, is forever, and the rewards there are everlasting.

- One courageous person can give many others the confidence to stand up for what they believe in.

- Just because one might not have children of their own, it does not mean that they cannot still be a parent by taking in and caring for children who are orphans or in need of help.

- Because of Aasiya's ﷺ generosity, she was blessed with much goodness: the pleasure of having a child that she could call her own, the pleasure of raising one of the greatest prophets in Islam, her death as a believer and as a martyr, and the miracle of seeing her palace in Jannah.

- We should never underestimate the power of du'a. Remember that Allah ﷻ sees and knows everything and will reward the ones who struggle in His path.

- Aasiya ؏ is an example to all those who believe. Even though she was the wife of one of the worst men on earth, she was still a woman of perfect faith.

- Sometimes we don't know what's going to happen in life. We don't know if or how we can overcome a situation. But if we keep our trust in Allah ﷻ, He will make a way out for us, just as He did when He reunited baby Musa with his birth mother.

Discussion Questions

1. Is it right to judge someone on the people they are surrounded by? Could this be wrong? How does the story of Aasiya ؏ demonstrate this?

2. Despite having physical beauty, wealth, status, and power, what meant most to Aasiya ؏? Which verse of the Qur'an mentions Aasiya ؏? What does she ask for, and what does it demonstrate about her faith?

3. What do you think it was like for Aasiya ؏ to have such an evil man as a husband?

4. What gave Aasiya ؏ the courage to stand up to Pharaoh, even though she was not as powerful as him?

5. What lessons from this incredible story can we apply to our lives?

Khadijah bint Khuwaylid

The Beloved First Wife of the Prophet ﷺ,
the First Mother of the Believers and the First Convert to Islam
6th century, Pre-Islamic Arabia

Khadijah ؓ was a powerful woman in the early history of Islam and continues to be one of the greatest role models for Muslim women today. Born around 555 CE, Khadijah ؓ was from the Banu Asad tribe of the Quraysh. She was the daughter of Khuwaylid ibn Asad, the leader of Banu Asad, and her mother was Fatima bint Za'idah.

People admired her righteousness and excellent character. Her personality was as beautiful as her appearance. She was called Ameerah al-Quraysh (the Princess of Quraysh), al-Tahira (the Pure One) and Khadijah al-Kubra (Khadijah the Great).

Khadijah ؓ was a wealthy woman who had been widowed twice. She was a loving mother and a savvy businesswoman. She used her keen intellectual abilities to amass great wealth, and she became the richest lady in Makkah.

Many men wished to wed Khadijah ؓ because of her beauty, noble qualities, high status, and wealth. However, Khadijah ؓ could not justify any of the proposals and instead focused on herself, raising her children and taking care of her business.

During this time, business records were rarely kept, and not many people could read or write. It was easy for unscrupulous individuals to lie about the sale price and keep most of the profit for themselves. Khadijah ﷺ was in desperate need of a trustworthy and reliable person whom she could hire to manage her business. Too often, she was cheated by those who were supposed to be responsible for her trades, and it was difficult for her to find someone she could trust.

Khadijah ﷺ had a sister named Hala, who owned camels and seeking to hire a reliable shepherd for her camels. She soon heard of a man known for his outstanding character and honesty. He was none other than Muhammad ﷺ, who was widely respected even before his prophethood. He was already known as al-Sadiq (the Honest) and al-Amin (the Trustworthy). Hala hired Muhammad ﷺ and another man immediately.

When the work was completed, Muhammad ﷺ felt shy to approach Hala for his wages and asked the man who worked with him to collect the money on his behalf. Hala enquired about Muhammad's ﷺ whereabouts, and the man explained the circumstances to her.

This news reached Khadijah ﷺ, and she was impressed by his humility. Surely a man who was too shy to collect his own wages was not greedy and would not cheat. She needed someone like him for her business. Khadijah ﷺ sent him a generous offer, asking him to be her business manager, and he accepted it. Muhammad ﷺ began to work for Khadijah ؓ. He made the largest profit anyone had ever made before him and gave it all to Khadijah ؓ.

Khadijah ؓ had never experienced such success in her business. Her servant Maysara went along with Muhammad ﷺ on trade trips and was amazed by his character. Maysara even witnessed miraculous occurrences: clouds that would shade Muhammad's ﷺ blessed head, and trees that bent over him whilst he was resting to protect him from the burning sun. He could tell that Muhammad ﷺ was a special man.

Khadijah ؓ heard only positive things about Muhammad ﷺ from her employees, servants and others. Through his dealings with her and her sister, she witnessed for herself the noble way in which Muhammad ﷺ carried himself. To her, Muhammad's ﷺ excellent qualities were worth more than any amount of money, for she had recognised that Muhammad ﷺ was truly rare and exceptional.

For the first time in a long time, Khadijah ؓ entertained the thought of marriage. She was wealthy, independent, strong, and powerful; even though Muhammad ﷺ wasn't rich and was younger than her, it didn't matter to her. What did matter was his impeccable character and sincere nature. Khadijah ؓ had declined marriage to the richest and most famous of men, but it was Muhammad ﷺ who impressed her. After learning about his honesty and witnessing his goodness, Khadijah ؓ desired to marry Muhammad ﷺ. She sent her servant Nafisah to tell Muhammad ﷺ of her wish, and he happily agreed to the marriage.

Soon after the marriage took place, a huge feast was held to celebrate the union. Thereafter, Muhammad ﷺ began living with Khadijah ؓ. Their marriage was celebrated by all the people of Makkah. They brought peace and happiness to one another. Their home was full of love and faith.

Muhammad ﷺ would often visit the cave of Hira to contemplate on the nature of society, the world, and the Divine. It was a place of peace and quiet. Hira was a long and exhausting walk from the Ka'bah, so he would camp there for a few days, or even up to a week at times. Khadijah ؓ would check on her beloved husband while he was at Hira. She would walk for hours before climbing up the steep mountain to finally reach the cave and nourish the soon-to-be prophet with food and water.

One day, whilst Muhammad ﷺ was engaged in his private reflections at Hira, an extraordinary event took place. Angel Jibreel ؑ appeared to him, commanding him to read! It was the moment Muhammed ﷺ received the first revelation from Allah ﷻ.

Muhammad ﷺ was quite shaken by this sudden encounter. Trembling in fear, he rushed back to his home, beseeching Khadijah ؓ to cover him up. She wrapped him in blankets and held him closely until he slowly calmed down. Muhammad ﷺ leaned into her embrace, confessing that he feared that he was going mad. When Khadijah ﷺ heard what had happened, she reassured him that everything was going to be all right. She reminded him of the mercy of Allah ﷻ. She recognised that Muhammad ﷺ was a man of sincerity and that Allah ﷻ was their protector. She soothed him with comforting words. 'No, by Allah, Allah will never disgrace you! You uphold the ties of kinship, you speak truthfully, you help the poor and destitute, you serve your guests generously and assist those who are struck by calamity' (*Sahih al-Bukhari*, 4572; *Sahih Muslim*, 231).

To make better sense of what had happened at the cave of Hira, Khadijah ﷺ decided to take Muhammad ﷺ to her wise cousin Waraqah. After listening closely to Muhammad's ﷺ story, Waraqah confirmed that the angel that came to him was indeed the same angel, Jibreel ﷺ, who had brought the revelations of Allah ﷻ to the Prophet Musa ﷺ.

Thus, Muhammad ﷺ became a prophet: a blessed messenger chosen by Allah ﷻ, sent as a mercy to the worlds. Khadijah ﷺ became the very first person to become a Muslim, bearing witness that there is none to be worshipped but Allah ﷻ and that Muhammad ﷺ is the Messenger of Allah ﷻ.

Muhammad ﷺ was instructed by Allah ﷻ to call people to monotheism. However, the leaders of the Quraysh rejected his invitation to worship the one true God (Allah). They made it difficult for people to accept Islam and for Muslims to live peacefully. They did everything in their power to stop the Prophet ﷺ from spreading his message. They were rude and cruel, insulting Muhammad ﷺ at every opportunity and making life for Muslims difficult.

Heartbroken, Muhammad ﷺ would share his sorrow with Khadijah ؓ, and she would comfort him lovingly. She had strong belief and trust in Allah ﷻ and would remind Muhammad ﷺ that surely Allah ﷻ would one day give him victory.

Khadijah ؓ was his strongest supporter. Khadijah's ؓ love for Muhammad ﷺ grew stronger and deeper. She had always believed in Allah ﷻ, and now she had the chance to do something great with her wealth and power for Allah's ﷻ pleasure. She spent all her wealth in the way of Allah ﷻ, helping to spread the message of Islam. She provided shelter and food for the growing number of new Muslims and used her money to free Muslim slaves. Her help was crucial to protecting and supporting the Muslims. She gave freely of everything she had and never hesitated or complained.

Khadijah ؓ and Muhammad ﷺ had a family of their own: two sons and four daughters. Sadly, their sons passed away during childhood. Nevertheless, Khadijah ؓ continued to be a maternal figure to all the Muslims in the most difficult of times. She helped new Muslims with her love, kindness, wealth, and support, always providing wisdom and valuable advice.

Her faith in Allah ﷻ and her caring approach renewed the resolve of everyone around her. *Umm al-Mu'mineen* – the Mother of the Believers – is a special title given to all the wives of Prophet Muhammad ﷺ; it demonstrates the love and respect we should have for them. Khadijah ﷺ was the first woman to be blessed with this title, and she lived up to it in every sense and until her last breath.

Khadijah ﷺ was a pious woman who was honoured by Allah ﷻ. Jibreel ﷺ once came to Muhammad ﷺ, and said: 'Allah's Messenger, Khadijah ﷺ is coming to you with a vessel of seasoned food or drink. When she comes to you, offer her greetings from her Lord, the Exalted and Glorious, and on my behalf, and give her glad tidings of a palace of jewels in Paradise wherein there is no noise and no toil' (*Sahih Muslim*, no. 2432). The fact that the greatest of angels, Jibreel ﷺ, was sent to deliver Allah's ﷻ salaam to Khadijah ﷺ demonstrates how truly special she was in the Sight of Allah. When Muhammad ﷺ shared Jibreel's ﷺ message with Khadijah ﷺ of this, she beautifully responded: 'Allah is al-Salaam (the giver of peace), and my salaam is upon Jibreel and upon you, Messenger of Allah. Salaam with the mercy and blessings of Allah' (*Sahih al-Bukhari*, no. 3364).

Khadijah ﷺ knew that spending all her wealth for the sake of Allah ﷻ would be worthwhile in the long term. When the Quraysh banished the Muslims to a barren valley and boycotted them as a punishment for their Islam, Khadijah ﷺ suffered alongside the Prophet ﷺ and the rest of the Muslims. By the time the boycott ended, Khadijah ﷺ was much older, and she died of the physical toll the starvation and hardship had taken on her body. Her last days were spent with Muhammad ﷺ and her beloved daughters. Khadijah ؑ lived with Muhammad ﷺ longer than any of his later wives, and she was his only wife during their marriage.

Sadly, Khadijah ؑ soon passed away. During the same year, Muhammad's ﷺ beloved uncle also passed away. It was an extremely difficult and painful year for the Prophet ﷺ, which came to be known as 'the Year of Sorrow'.

Although Muhammad ﷺ later remarried, but his love for Khadijah ؑ never faded. He would talk about her fondly and often; whenever he was gifted with food, he would send some of it to Khadijah's ؑ neighbours and friends. If a friend of Khadijah ؑ visited Muhammad ﷺ, he was extremely welcoming and kind to her. He missed Khadijah ؑ dearly, even long after she had passed away. When Khadijah's ؑ sister, Hala, came to visit, the Prophet's ﷺ whole body language changed; in Hala's voice, he recognised her sister, and it was almost as if Khadijah ؑ was there with them.

One time, when he came across Khadijah's ؑ necklace, his grief was visible; it brought back many beloved memories of their time together. Even though Khadijah ؑ was gone, her memory lived on forever in the mind and heart of the Prophet ﷺ. The Prophet's ﷺ love for Khadijah ؑ was intense, and he missed her terribly.

When Muhammad ﷺ mentioned four of the best women to enter Paradise, he mentioned Khadijah ؑ as one of them. Khadijah ؑ the Great was a friend, adviser, supporter, believer,

Khadijah bint Khuwaylid

and comforter of the Prophet ﷺ. This is how Muhammad ﷺ described his beloved Khadijah ﷺ in a hadith: 'She had faith in me when people rejected me. She believed in me when the people disbelieved in me. She supported me with her wealth when the people prevented me. And Allah blessed me with children through her and not through any other wife' (*Sahih al-Bukhari*, no. 3821). Just as she remained in the Prophet's ﷺ heart, our own hearts should be filled with love for her and what she did for our Ummah. Our beloved mother, Khadijah bint Khuwaylid ﷺ, was truly an extraordinary woman, and she will forever remain a role model for girls and women everywhere.

Reflections
- In her time, it was unusual for a woman to run a business, but Khadijah ﷺ achieved her goals with confidence and great success. We should not be afraid of trying something new, even if it's daunting at first, as long as it is lawful in Islam.
- Khadijah ﷺ financed the Islamic movement. She was a part of a small Muslim community, but she did whatever she could to help the Muslims.

REMARKABLE *Muslim Women*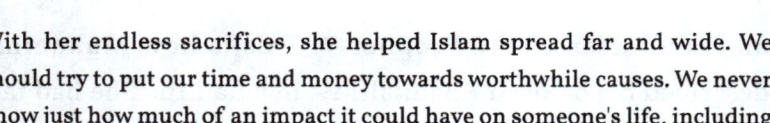

With her endless sacrifices, she helped Islam spread far and wide. We should try to put our time and money towards worthwhile causes. We never know just how much of an impact it could have on someone's life, including our own in this world or in the hereafter.

- A lady of maturity, wisdom and nobility, Khadijah ؓ proved to be the Prophet Muhammad's ﷺ greatest friend and a beacon of love for him. The fact that she had been married twice before and had children from a previous marriage did not factor into the Prophet's decision to marry her. Therefore, we should try to stay open-minded and not stigmatise anyone and try to see the good in every opportunity.

- When we experience Islamophobia, we should take inspiration from our mother Khadijah ؓ and never give up our faith to fear. We need to pave the way for others after us through our resilience and endurance in the face of hardship like Khadijah ؓ did. By continuing to strive to please Allah ﷻ in the face of hate, we will be successful, God willing.

- Muhammad ﷺ loved Khadijah ؓ dearly. He never forgot her, and he kept her memory alive. When our loved ones return to Allah ﷻ, we should try to keep their memories alive too by honouring their family and friends, by keeping in touch with them, showing kindness towards them and welcoming them or sending them food or gifts like the Prophet ﷺ did.

Discussion Questions

1. What made Khadijah ؓ so remarkable? What do you think was her greatest trait?

2. What was the special quality of Muhammad ﷺ that impressed Khadijah ؓ the most, and why was this quality equally important for her business and her marriage?

3. In a world that glorifies wealth and power, what does Khadijah's ؓ story teach us?

4. Why is it important to build or start something good, even though we may not get to see the long-term results of our efforts?

Aisha bint Abu Bakr

A Great Scholar and Mother of the Believers

7th century, Arabia

Aisha ؓ was the daughter of Abu Bakr al-Siddeeq ؓ, the best friend of the Prophet ﷺ. After his wife Khadijah ؓ died, Muhammad ﷺ married Aisha ؓ. She held a unique place in his heart. In fact, the Prophet ﷺ said the most beloved person to him was Aisha ؓ, and then her father.

An outspoken young woman, Aisha ؓ was brave, intelligent, and a great leader. Her vast knowledge meant that she was a confident speaker. She was respectful yet did not shy away from speaking when she had something on her mind. Her husband ﷺ lovingly called her *Humaira*, which means 'the one with a reddish complexion'.

Aisha and Muhammad ﷺ were happily married and loved to be in each other's company. We know details about the Prophet's ﷺ private life, such as how he slept, how he took a bath and so much more because of Aisha ؓ.

Aisha ؓ had a good sense of humour and a fun-loving relationship with the Prophet ﷺ. They loved to joke, laugh, and play with one another. They would race together; the first time they did, Aisha ﷺ won. But the second time, she lost, and the Prophet ﷺ would tease her about it often. They had a strong romantic connection. Whenever the Prophet ﷺ would leave for the masjid, he would kiss Aisha ﷺ. They would eat from the same dish and drink from the same cup – each drinking in the exact same place the other had drunk from.

The Prophet ﷺ was always patient and had time for Aisha ﷺ. Once, when they were traveling on a military expedition, Aisha ﷺ lost a necklace. Distraught, she told the Prophet ﷺ and he ordered the entire army to stop and search for the necklace. As the time for Fajr approached, the Muslims were concerned about missing the prayer due to lack of water for ablution. It was during this time Allah revealed the verses of Tayammum, enabling the Muslims to pray with an alternative method of purification.

Aisha ﷺ was a chaste woman who never behaved immodestly. Yet one sad day, she realised that a huge lie was spread about her. All throughout the city, people were accusing her of something terrible that she did not do! When Aisha ﷺ learned of this, she cried. It upset her, and she went through a difficult time. Yet she kept strong in her faith in Allah ﷻ, the One who knew of her innocence, because He ﷻ has knowledge of everything. She chose to be patient and sought Allah's ﷻ help, certain that He ﷻ would prove her innocence. Indeed, Allah's ﷻ help came! He ﷻ revealed the truth in Surah An-Nur, 24:11.

Aisha ﷺ praised Allah ﷻ. The Prophet ﷺ then went out to the people and informed them what Allah ﷻ had revealed in the Qur'an about Aisha ﷺ. The people who were responsible for the lies were punished.

During her marriage to the Prophet, the fearless Aisha ﷺ participated in the biggest battles against the Quraysh. She brought water for the Muslim warriors and helped to look after the wounded.

Despite the hard times of poverty and hunger that the Prophet ﷺ and Aisha ﷺ endured, she remained extremely generous. For months, the Prophet ﷺ and Aisha ﷺ survived on only dates and water. Aisha ﷺ chose the simple life because she desired Allah ﷻ, His Messenger ﷺ and the eternal life of the hereafter. Once, when she was fasting, she received a gift of one hundred thousand dirhams. She gave this money to the poor and needy, despite having no food or other items in her own house. She didn't think for a moment of her own needs!

Aisha ﷺ earned the nickname 'the Mother of Fragrance' because whenever a beggar knocked on her door, she would add a touch of perfume to the money before handing it over. She said she knew the charity would reach Allah ﷻ before it reached the beggar's hands, and she wanted it to be given to Allah ﷻ in a sweet and fragrant condition. Aisha ﷺ gave what she could. One day, when a needy person knocked on her door, she only had one grape and gave it away. She understood that every good deed – no matter how small – should be done for the pleasure of Allah ﷻ.

She understood from the Qur'an that whoever does an atom's weight of good will see it, and whoever does an atom's weight of evil will see it.

During the last days of the Prophet's ﷺ life, while he was ill, he wanted to stay close to Aisha ؓ. His beloved wife took great care of him. The Prophet ﷺ passed away while resting on her lap and was buried in her house. This was a true honour for her.

Aisha ؓ continued speaking of her beloved husband Muhammad ﷺ lovingly till the day she died, forty-six years later. She had no complaints against him, and it was Aisha ؓ who relayed the most detailed information about the Prophet's ﷺ life in the hadith.

Although Aisha ؓ was young and beautiful, her greatest strength was not her physical beauty but her righteous character. She was generous and kind and had an extraordinary talent for absorbing knowledge. This characteristic made her an excellent teacher and a conveyor of sacred knowledge about the Prophet ﷺ and the Qur'an. She was able to narrate the life and sayings of the Prophet ﷺ in great detail and she had incredible knowledge of the magnificent Qur'an.

Aisha ؓ was one of the greatest teachers in the history of Islam. Through her sharp memory and attention to detail, she taught many great male and female scholars the knowledge that we treasure to this day. Whenever those of great knowledge had questions related to the Prophet ﷺ or the Qur'an, they would ask Aisha ؓ. It was during the Prophet's marriage to her that the teachings of Islam were perfected and completed. Aisha ؓ not only lived the Sunnah, but also memorised the entire Qur'an by heart and lived by it.

Much of Aisha's ؓ knowledge was preserved by later scholars in Islamic texts. Aisha ؓ is one of only four people who have transmitted more than two thousand hadiths.

After the passing of the Messenger of Allah ﷺ and during her long life, Aisha ؓ became the teacher of scholars. One of the most famous companions of the Prophet ﷺ, 'Umar ibn al-Khattab ؓ, confessed he would have been lost on every issue, big or small, during his own caliphate without Aisha's ؓ valuable advice.

Aisha ؓ returned to Allah ﷻ in the month of Ramadan. She did not have children of her own, but she is known as 'Umm al-Mu'minin' (Mother of the Believers). She had a life of great purpose and left behind an unparalleled legacy. Important Islamic books about the Qur'an, biographies of the Prophet Muhammad ﷺ, and detailed jurisprudence all include Aisha's ؓ name as a reference. Aisha ؓ was extremely important amongst her contemporaries as well as generations to come. Aisha ؓ is a perfect example for every Muslim girl and woman. She was devoted to Allah ﷻ and was a righteous leader and educator.

The Prophet ﷺ said, 'Many men reached perfection but none among the women reached perfection except Maryam, the daughter of Imran, and Aasiya, Pharoah's wife. And the superiority of Aisha to other women is like the superiority of thareed to other kinds of food' (*Sahih al-Bukhari*, no. 5418). *Thareed was used as an example because it was the best meal for Arabs at that time and no other dish was superior to it. In other words, just as thareed is the best of food, then Aisha ﷺ is the best of women.*

Reflections

- Aisha ﷺ was the most distinguished scholar of her time who memorised the perfect book of Allah ﷻ. She was also well-versed in interpreting the Qur'an's meanings. Could there be a better goal for us to emulate? Like Aisha ﷺ, we should aim to dedicate our lives to memorising the Qur'an and being students of knowledge, God willing. With the help of Allah ﷻ, anything is possible.

- We should use whatever knowledge and skills we have to benefit the Ummah and the world at large. Our contributions may become an ongoing charity for us after we have returned home to our Lord.

- Aisha ﷺ did not bear any children of her own, yet she is a perfect example of a great woman. She displayed all the qualities of a loving mother with the care she provided to those around her, from men and women of high positions to the destitute.

- People can be mean. When we feel hurt by lies or when we feel alone and misunderstood, we should trust in Allah ﷻ and have sabr (patience), as Aisha ﷺ did. Allah ﷻ will help us through any hardship if we pray and practise patience. We are never alone when we have Allah ﷻ.

Aisha bint Abu Bakr

- Aisha ﷺ had a fun-loving and romantic relationship with her spouse ﷺ. We should pray for a beautiful future filled with beautiful relationships.

- It must have been completely heart-breaking for Aisha ﷺ to lose the love of her life, her beloved husband ﷺ, at such a young age. However, she did not despair, and she carried on with his legacy. When we lose the ones we love, we should take comfort in knowing that the believers will be with the ones they love in Jannah. Goodbyes are only temporary in this world. We should strive to continue the legacy of those who have passed before us with good deeds that will please Allah ﷺ.

- Aisha ﷺ did everything with excellence. We should put our best efforts forth, even if they may not be good enough for others. God willing, they will be accepted by Allah ﷺ, as He knows of our capabilities and our limitations. The world may criticise us, but if we are sincere, then our Lord will reward us tremendously, God willing.

- It is recommended to give charity to one who is in need, even if it is something small. The Prophet ﷺ said: 'Protect yourselves from the fire even if it is with half a date' (*Sahih al-Bukhari*, no. 5564; *Sahih Muslim*, no.1689).

Discussion Questions

1. How would you describe Aisha's ﷺ personality?

2. Do you think everyone matures at the same age?

3. How do you think Aisha ﷺ felt about her blessed husband, Muhammad ﷺ? How would you describe their marriage?

4. What were her contributions to society and the Muslim world?

5. Have you ever wanted to give charity but hesitated because what you had was 'too small'?

Rufaida al-Aslamiyyah

A Social Worker and Expert Healer

7th century, Arabia

Rufaida al-Aslamiyyah ﷻ was born in Yathrib in the Arabian Peninsula in the time of the Prophet ﷺ. She was a caring and hard-working woman with a noble personality. Her father, Saad al-Aslamy, was a famous healer, and he taught his daughter to care for the sick and wounded. Rufaida's ﷻ father inspired her to work in healthcare so that she could take care of the ill and injured and help them heal. Rufaida ﷻ was not only a brilliant healer, but also an excellent teacher who trained other women to become healers as well.

Rufaida's ﷻ family was among the first in Yathrib to accept Islam and to welcome Prophet Muhammad ﷺ into the city. When Prophet Muhammad ﷺ and his army were leaving for the Battle of Khaybar, Rufaida ﷻ and her group of volunteer healers sought permission to go with him to treat the injured Muslims and give water to the thirsty. Acknowledging the need for such a vital service, the Prophet ﷺ granted his permission. Rufaida ﷻ was an excellent organiser and leader. On the battlefield, she protected the wounded and dying from the desert wind and heat by providing shelter in her tent, which was set up for that purpose. She was always prepared to provide her service during wartime, moving her tent from one battleground to another.

Rufaida's ﷺ tent can be compared to what is known today as a field hospital – a temporary hospital set up near a battlefield to provide emergency care for the wounded. She paid all the expenses needed to provide this service and never took any wages. She sought the reward of Allah ﷻ alone. She and the other healers did such an outstanding job that Muhammad ﷺ gave them a reward for the incredible service they had provided. Although they were rewarded by the Prophet ﷺ out of gratitude, Rufaida ﷺ and the other nurses didn't help the wounded with the hopes of earning money. They did it for free, seeking the reward of Allah ﷻ alone.

Rufaida ﷺ became well known for looking after the wounded during battles. In times of peace, the Prophet Muhammad ﷺ gave her permission to erect a tent inside the masjid (al-Masjid al-Nabawi) in Madinah so that she could continue her medical practice. She also trained more Muslim women to become healers. When a companion of the Prophet ﷺ had a deep wound in his arm after being struck with a spear, the Prophet ﷺ said, 'Let him stay in Rufaida's tent in the masjid until I return'.

Rufaida's ﷺ treatment of the sick and wounded in her tent provided safety and comfort and an unobtrusive place for patients to recover. Rufaida ﷺ had a curious mind and wanted

to learn more about diseases and their causes. She worked in poor communities, trying to improve the level of hygiene and to eradicate poverty, both of which strongly affect health. She thought of ways to prevent disease and taught them to others.

Rufaida ﷺ was both a healer and a social worker. She helped children in need and took care of the poor, orphans and people with disabilities. She devoted her life to healing the sick. In serving her community, she was serving her faith. What a remarkable woman!

Reflections

- A good Muslim works towards bettering themselves, their family, and their community if they have the capacity to do so.

- There is nothing wrong with earning money for our time or with being wealthy. In fact, having wealth allows us to contribute and benefit others. But whatever good we do, we should renew our intentions and strive to be sincere to earn the pleasure of our Creator. And if we can, we should aim to give of our time or skills freely, especially if it will benefit the ummah.

- In Islam, women receive the same rewards for deeds as men. Both the men

REMARKABLE Muslim Women

and women who served in the army for the sake of Allah, regardless of how they contributed, were praised and rewarded by the Prophet ﷺ.

- When we give for the sake of Allah ﷻ, He ﷻ gives something better back to us.

- Rufaida's ؓ tent was a much-needed service to help the Muslims on the battlefield. With a bit of creativity, anything is possible. Creativity can lead to endless opportunities to open doors and change the way the world works, God willing!

- The Prophet ﷺ said: 'Whoever is focused only on this world, Allah will confound his affairs and make him fear poverty constantly, and he will not get anything of this world except that which has been decreed for him. Whoever is focused on the hereafter, Allah will settle his affairs for him and make him feel content with his lot, and his provision and worldly gains will undoubtedly come to him' (*Sunan Ibn Majah*, no. 4105).
Rufaida ؓ did not chase fame. She became famous due to her beneficial work, and her worldly affairs were taken care of by Allah ﷻ. We must renew our intentions and not let the desire for fame darken our hearts. If we do actions for the right reasons, then we will be content like Rufaida ؓ was.

Discussion Questions

1. What influence did Rufaida's ؓ father have on her?

2. What do you think motivated Rufaida ؓ to carry out the beneficial work that she did?

3. In which way was Rufaida ؓ innovative?

4. How did her work help Muslims?

5. Can you think of ways to help someone you know?

6. Do you know what the Qur'an says about saving a life?

7. How can fame have a negative impact on some people, and what is your advice to them?

Nusayba bint Ka'ab

A Fierce Warrior and Loyal Companion of the Prophet ﷺ

7th century, Arabia

Nusayba bint Ka'ab ؓ, also known as Umm Ammarah, was a member of the Banu Najjar tribe from the Ansar of Yathrib. She had two sons – Abdullah and Habib – from her first marriage and a son and daughter – Tamim and Khawlah – from her second marriage. She was a loving mother and wife.

In the early days of Islam, Muslims in Makkah were subjected to harsh treatment and torture by the Makkans. They often faced hardship and severe persecution. Islam gave equal rights to men, women and slaves. The Makkans were full of pride and arrogance and thought they were better than everyone else. They considered the Muslim belief in one God and equal rights for all a betrayal of their forefathers, who believed in multiple gods and superiority over others.

Eventually, the Prophet ﷺ met a group of people from Yathrib led by As'ad ibn Zurara of the Khazraj tribe and invited them to Islam. They gladly accepted. Thereafter, the Prophet Muhammad ﷺ sent his companion Musab ibn 'Umayr to Yathrib to spread the noble message of Islam.

Praise be to Allah ﷻ, the message was welcomed and embraced by almost all the tribes in Yathrib. Afterwards, Yathrib was renamed Madinah al-Nabi (the City of the Prophet). Once rivals, the tribes of Madinah were eventually united as a single Muslim community. They were known as the Ansar: the Helpers of Islam and the Prophet ﷺ.

When the blessed message reached Nusayba's ؓ ears and heart, she embraced Islam with every fibre of her being. Eventually, seventy-two men and two women travelled from Madinah to Mount al-Aqabah in Makkah to swear allegiance to Islam. To avoid danger from the enemy, they secretly met the Prophet Muhammad ﷺ at night to make the pledge.

The Prophet ﷺ was informed by Nusayba's ؓ husband that two women also wanted to swear allegiance to him and Allah. He gladly accepted their pledge. He informed them that equal terms would apply to the women and men, except that he shook only men's hands, and not the women's, due to Islamic protocol.

Nusayba ؓ and Asma bint 'Amr ؓ were the only two women to personally witness this momentous event and to pledge directly to the Prophet ﷺ. Their participation came at a great risk because if they were caught, they could have been persecuted or killed.

This swearing of allegiance to the Prophet ﷺ is called *Bay'ah al-Aqabah al-Thaniyah*. It was the second oath in Islamic history.

Nusayba's ؓ life had changed forever. The impact of

pledging to the Prophet ﷺ directly gave her a higher purpose in life. Her new dedication to Islam imbued her body with renewed passion and filled her soul with joy. It strengthened her further in faith, and on her return to Madinah, she eagerly devoted herself to the education of women. She began teaching Islam and became a charismatic leader and educator in her community. She would perform prayers in the masjid and attend religious lessons.

Nusayba ؓ reflected a great deal on the Qur'an and the way it spoke about gender roles. One day she asked the Prophet ﷺ, 'Why is the Qur'an addressed directly to men?' The answer then came directly from Allah ﷻ. An entire verse was revealed in the Qur'an to answer Nusayba's ؓ question in Surah al-Ahzab (the Confederates):

> *Muslim men and Muslim women, believing men and believing women, obedient men and obedient women, truthful men and truthful women, patient men and patient women, humble men and humble women, charitable men and charitable women, fasting men and fasting women, men who guard their chastity and women who guard, men who remember God frequently and women who remember — God has prepared for them a pardon, and an immense reward.* Qur'an, 33:35

By the grace of Allah ﷻ, Nusayba ؓ had helped to clarify the position of Islam on women, which brought reassurance and contentment to the hearts and lives of many people. Before Islam, the Arabs did not value women and even buried their own daughters alive just because of their gender. Islam changed all this and gave equal rights and value to girls and women. Nusayba ﷺ had an excellent memory and used to memorise the words of the Prophet ﷺ, the hadith, and teach them to others. She played a major role in society as an important narrator of hadith.

The Makkan tribes were infuriated by the growth of Islam and by their loss of the Battle of Badr. They had prepared for a long time to launch a surprise attack on the Muslims and had carefully planned every move. However, Allah supported the Muslims, despite their small numbers, and they were victorious over the Quraysh. The Makkans could not accept this defeat, and they attacked a second time at the Battle of Uhud.

The Prophet ﷺ had given the soldiers at the Battle of Uhud strict orders to not leave their positions, no matter what. At first, the Muslims were winning the battle. But when the archers on the hill saw the other soldiers collecting the war booty and the enemies nowhere in sight, they thought that the battle was over. Some of them disobeyed the Prophet ﷺ and abandoned their positions. Consequently, chaos erupted, and the tide turned against the Muslims. When the fleeing Makkans saw that most of the archers had retreated and that the Muslims were scattered, they took this as an opportunity to launch a sudden attack when the Muslims were least expecting it. The Muslims were defeated despite their near victory.

Sadly, many elder companions were martyred. The Prophet

Nusayba bint Ka'ab

ﷺ himself incurred various injuries. He broke a molar tooth and bled profusely from injuries to his face.

Nusayba ؓ accompanied the Prophet ﷺ and the Muslims to the Battle of Uhud. Like many other female companions, Nusayba ؓ was tasked with providing water to thirsty soldiers in the intense heat. She also helped nurse those wounded in the battle.

Nusayba ؓ was holding a vessel of water in her hands when she saw that the Prophet ﷺ was in danger. She immediately grabbed a sword from a fleeing soldier and a bow and arrows from another and rushed to defend the Prophet ﷺ. Nusayba ؓ was a fearless warrior! She struck fatal blows to her opponents and shielded the Prophet ﷺ so that no harm would come to him. She protected him from every direction. Her love and concern for the Prophet ﷺ made her fearless of the enemy and uninterested in her own safety. Nusayba ؓ, along with her husband and two valiant sons, surrounded the Prophet ﷺ to protect him from attackers from every corner.

When the Prophet ﷺ saw an enemy coming closer to harm Nusayba ؓ, he called upon her son to protect her. Her voice strong with unwavering faith, Nusayba ؓ called out to the Prophet ﷺ. 'Oh Messenger of Allah ﷻ, invoke Allah ﷻ to make us your companions in Paradise!' When Nusayba ؓ saw her son bleeding heavily, she wrapped a bandage on his arm and told him not to lose hope, urging him to continue fighting with all his might.

The Prophet ﷺ smiled when he saw this and said, 'Where can one get courage like yours, oh Umm Ammarah?' Impressed by her heroism and unrelenting dedication, he made dua. The Messenger of Allah supplicated, 'Oh Allah ﷻ, make them my companions in the Garden!' Nusayba ؓ was overjoyed to hear this, as going to Jannah with the Prophet ﷺ was her only desire. The Muslim soldiers were amazed by Nusayba's ؓ fighting skills, spirit, and determination.

Nusayba ؓ used her own body to shield the Prophet ﷺ from a line of arrows that were fired at him. At one point, she was seriously injured and fell unconscious. It is said that her first question when she woke up was, 'Did the Prophet survive?' Nusayba ؓ was inflicted with multiple severe wounds on the battlefield. She suffered a deep stab wound to her shoulder, which she continued to struggle with for the rest of her life.

The Prophet ﷺ once told 'Umar ibn al-Khattab ؓ that in the Battle of Uhud, wherever he turned, he saw Umm Ammarah fighting in his defence. The Companions of the Prophet ﷺ held Nusayba ؓ in high esteem due to her valour. Despite her deep wounds and suffering, Nusayba ؓ never had regrets. She bore her wounds as a medal of pride and proudly told the story of how she gained the scars on her body. Serving Islam and defending the Prophet ﷺ had resulted in many physical injuries, but it had healed her soul and increased her in love for Allah ﷻ.

Nusayba's ؓ patience and courage went beyond the battlefield. She experienced heartbreak from losing her two beloved sons when they were martyred. The death of her son Habeeb, who was a gentle young man and the apple of his mother's eye, was particularly dreadful and gruesome. A man named Musaylamah, who pretended to be a prophet, wanted her son Habeeb to bear witness to his prophethood. When Habeeb refused to comply, Musaylamah the Liar ordered Habeeb to be tortured. His limbs were cut off one by one until he died.

When the Prophet ﷺ, Abu Bakr al-Siddeeq ؓ and 'Umar ؓ informed Nusayba ؓ of the tragic death of her beloved son, she showed exemplary patience after receiving consolation from the Prophet ﷺ. She demonstrated utmost dignity and grace at a time when she was overwhelmed by both physical and emotional pain. However, Nusayba ؓ felt the pain of grief once again when the Prophet ﷺ passed away. She soothed herself by remembering the prayer of the Prophet ﷺ and knowing that her family would be reunited with him ﷺ in Paradise.

Abu Bakr al-Siddeeq ؓ was unanimously appointed the new Muslim ruler. He informed Nusayba ؓ, who was now in her sixties and feeble, of an upcoming battle to challenge Musaylamah the Liar and his army. Despite her age and the pain she still felt from her previous wounds, she insisted on going with them. Her other son, Abdullah ibn Zaid, went with her. During the battle, Nusayba ؓ fought fearlessly with all her might. Sadly, she was seriously wounded once again. Her left arm was cut off at the shoulder, at the site of an old wound. Nusayba's ؓ spirit was buoyed because she knew that if she was martyred, she would be reunited in Paradise with those she loved. She was so engrossed in fighting that she did not even realise that she had lost an arm! Suddenly she heard that Musaylamah the Liar, who had mercilessly killed her son Habeeb, had been struck by a spear. Along with her son Abdullah, Nusayba ﷺ rushed to exact her revenge. This battle was called the Battle of Yamamah. The Prophet's ﷺ blessed prayer for her became a source of patience in the final years of her life and gave her some ease during her hardships.

Nusayba lived through the rule of Abu Bakr al-Siddeeq ﷺ and 'Umar ibn al-Khattab ﷺ. She was honoured by both *khulafaa'*, and they commended her sacrifices and bravery. During his rule, 'Umar ibn al-Khattab ﷺ received a beautiful gift: a piece of cloth made from the finest silk. Some companions suggested that it should be given to his daughter or daughter-in-law. 'Umar ﷺ said that he knew of someone who was more deserving of it than anyone else and sent it to Nusayba ﷺ.

Nusayba ﷺ was a heroic warrior who fought for justice and was not afraid for her own safety, especially when it came to defending the Prophet ﷺ from attackers. She was regarded highly by the Prophet ﷺ and by great companions. She was confident enough to ask about the role of women in Islam; due to her zeal for knowledge, a verse was revealed in the magnificent Qur'an. Nusayba ﷺ was a renowned woman of extraordinary strength and faith. She was a woman of great confidence, patience and sacrifice, and fiercely protective of the Prophet ﷺ.

Nusayba bint Ka'ab

Nusayba ؓ is a role model and real-life superhero for every girl, woman, boy and man. Nusayba died in AH 13 and was buried in Makkah.

Reflections

- A person should be judged by their merit and credentials, and not by their gender. Nusayba ؓ proved herself as a worthy warrior and was revered by everyone around her. Islam teaches us that women and men are not the same, and although we may have different responsibilities, we all deserve to be treated fairly and in accordance with Islam. Islam is a way of life, and it contains a perfect framework for life and society. After he embraced Islam, 'Umar ibn al-Khattab ؓ said: 'In Jahiliyya, we used to have no regard for women whatsoever. But when Islam came and Allah made mention of them, this caused us to realise that they have rights upon us' (*Sahih al-Bukhari*, no. 5505).

- At the Battle of Uhud, when the archers disobeyed the order of the Prophet ﷺ by abandoning their positions, it turned the tide for the Muslims. If we have committed to being part of a team, we should do our part and fulfil our role. Neglecting our duty can lead to grave consequences.

- Obeying the Prophet ﷺ and Allah ﷻ is just as important today as it was for the Muslim army at the Battle of Uhud. We can do this by following the Qur'an and Sunnah as closely as possible and by refraining from anything

prohibited. We will eventually feel the positive effects of obeying Allah ﷻ and his Messenger ﷺ rather than the negative effects of disobeying them in this life and in the hereafter.

- If we have a question, then we should ask someone with knowledge. We should have the courage to speak up. However, we should do so respectfully, and we should not feel bad for trying to understand. We should do whatever we can to educate ourselves by gaining more knowledge.

- Like Nusayba ؓ, we can still defend the Prophet ﷺ and Islam today - not with weapons, but by being the best in character and speech. By sharing information about who the Prophet ﷺ truly was, we can illustrate what Islam truly is.

- We can express our love for the Prophet ﷺ by striving to follow Islam and by following his beloved Sunnah and sending *salawaat* on him.

- Failure does not mean permanent defeat. In every failure, there is a lesson to be learned. Although the Muslims were defeated in the Battle of Uhud, they learned important lessons, and in the end they were victorious.

- Nusayba ؓ would pray in the masjid. Women have prayed in Masjids since the time of the Prophet ﷺ and continue to do so today. This includes Masjid al-Nabawi, established and originally built by the Prophet himself. The Prophet Muhammad ﷺ said, 'Do not prevent the female servants of Allah from the masjids of Allah' (*Sahih Muslim*, no. 442). So when you hear of people discouraging women to pray at the masjid, be aware of the God given rights of a Muslim woman to worship at the masjid.

Discussion Questions
1. How did Islam transform how women were viewed? How did it raise women to a position of prominence and dignity?

2. How was Nusayba ؓ motivated by her faith?

Nusayba bint Ka'ab

3. How did the Prophet ﷺ and the most prominent companions treat and honour Nusayba ؟

4. What do you think made Nusayba so fearless and bold?

5. What was Nusayba most famous for?

Fatima al-Fihri

The Founder of the World's Oldest University

9th century, Ifriqiyyah

Fatima was born in Ifriqiyyah (in modern-day Tunisia), and her family later moved to Fez, Morocco. Fatima was a kind-hearted girl and the daughter of a wealthy businessman called Mohammad al-Fihri. The family was so rich that they were like royalty. Fatima had a sister called Mariam, and their father loved them both very much. He made sure that they got only the best in education. Fatima and Mariam loved to learn, pray, and read the Qur'an.

When Fatima grew up, she married a wealthy man. Sadly, sometime later, Fatima's husband and father both passed away. *Inna lillahi wa inna ilayhi raji'un*: Surely, to Allah ﷺ we belong, and to Him we return.

Fatima and Mariam were now left with a huge inheritance. They realised that they had the power to do a lot of good for their community, so they brainstormed different ways to help others. Fatima and her sister had always been interested in supporting Islamic education and architecture. As the two sisters put their heads together, they came up with a brilliant new idea!

They decided to build a masjid where people could not only pray but also gain Islamic knowledge. This was their chance to make their lifelong dream come true. Fatima spent all of her inheritance in building a masjid called al-Qarawiyyin. She named the masjid after her birth city in Ifriqiyyah. Similarly, Mariam spent her money building the al-Andalus Masjid.

The work on the al-Qarawiyyin Masjid began in Ramadan. Fatima was very much involved in the work. She hired local workers and used local materials and supervised the construction herself. Fatima took care of her workers by building a well next to the construction site so that they would have easy access to water.

Fatima's intention behind this entire project was for the sake of Allah, and she wanted it to receive His blessings. As a sign of her commitment, she vowed to fast until the work on the masjid was completed. When the final brick was laid, the first thing Fatima did was pray two units of prayer to express her thankfulness to Allah ﷻ for answering her prayers and making her dream come true.

Fatima decided to add an institute of learning to the masjid. Anybody who studied there had their room, board and books covered by the endowment established by Fatima al-Fihri. This meant they could study for free, without the worry of student debt. Her generosity ensured that the less advantaged could benefit from an education that they otherwise may not have had access to. Together with Qur'an and jurisprudence, students

learned medicine, mathematics, astronomy, chemistry, and the humanities.

Fatima ensured that this education was made available to people of all ages, social classes, and faiths. The masjid grew bigger and bigger until it became one of the largest universities in the whole world and the first educational institution to award degrees. The al-Qarawiyyin university predates the oldest European university by almost two centuries.

Al-Qarawiyyin opened its doors in 857 CE and is now considered the oldest university in the world. It is still one of the greatest landmarks of the country and continues to encourage learning and education even today. Many famous individuals studied at the university, including the historian Ibn Khaldun, the astronomer and jurist al-Bitruji (known as Alpetragius in Europe), the renowned Jewish physician, theologian and philosopher Maimonedes; and Gerbert d'Aurillac, who became Pope Sylvester II (the first French pope and the scientist who introduced zero and the Arabic numerals to Europe). The al-Qarawiyyin library was also founded by Fatima al-Fihri and is the oldest library in the world. The library was recently restored by architect and Fez native, Aziza Chaouni, and it is now open to the public. One of the treasures in the library is a ninth-century Qur'an, written in Kufic (the oldest form of Arabic calligraphy) on camel skin.

Fatima al-Fihri was a pious young woman. Fatima understood that the way to fulfilling dreams was to be persistent in her supplications, to increase her good deeds and to work hard and be patient. She was a mover and shaker who inspired people to seek education and achieve greatness. She had a significant impact on the development of the city of Fez. Fatima's dedication to her project essentially made her the woman behind some of history's intellectual giants. Her vision illuminated the path of those who came after her. She was charitable, generous, selfless and a true pioneer and visionary. She put the pleasure of Allah ﷻ before her personal pleasure, sacrificing her money to fulfil her vision. Before women were allowed an education in most places in the world, Fatima al-Fihri set up an educational institution of her own. She was a phenomenal woman and everyone who values education should value her contribution to the world. Fatima and Mariam's diplomas can be found hanging on the wall in the upper chamber of Al-Qarawiyyin even today.

Reflections
- Sincerity and acts of goodness always pay off.
- If we really want something, then we should increase our good deeds, like

giving charity or fasting for the pleasure of Allah ﷻ.

- No matter what our circumstances are, we should never give up. Even though Fatima lost her father and her husband, she never lost hope. She did everything in her power to make the world around her a better place.

- We should always be kind and think of others. Fatima inherited a large amount from her father, but she didn't keep it all to herself. Instead, she generously shared her wealth with her community and left behind a great legacy.

- We should try to increase our knowledge (especially knowledge that brings us closer to our Creator) and to make the path of knowledge easy for others in any way that we can. The Prophet ﷺ said that 'seeking knowledge is an obligation upon every Muslim' (*Sunan Ibn Majah*, no. 224).

- It is mentioned in a hadith that 'the rewards of the good deeds that will reach a believer after his death are: knowledge that he taught and spread, a righteous son whom he leaves behind, a copy of the Qur'an that he leaves as a legacy, a mosque that he built, a house that he built for wayfarers, a canal that he dug, or charity that he gave during his lifetime when he was in good health. These deeds will reach him after his death' (*Sunan Ibn Majah*, no. 242).

Discussion Questions

1. In what ways can we express our gratitude to Allah ﷻ?
2. Is simply making dua enough if we want to achieve our dreams? Why?
3. If people don't believe in us or feel that our goals are strange, should we give up on them?
4. Which part of the story shows that Fatima cared for her employees? How do you think it made them feel, and what impact do you think it had on their performance?

5. Do you need to be wealthy in order to please Allah or to do something of benefit?
6. Have Muslim women always contributed to their society, or is this something new?

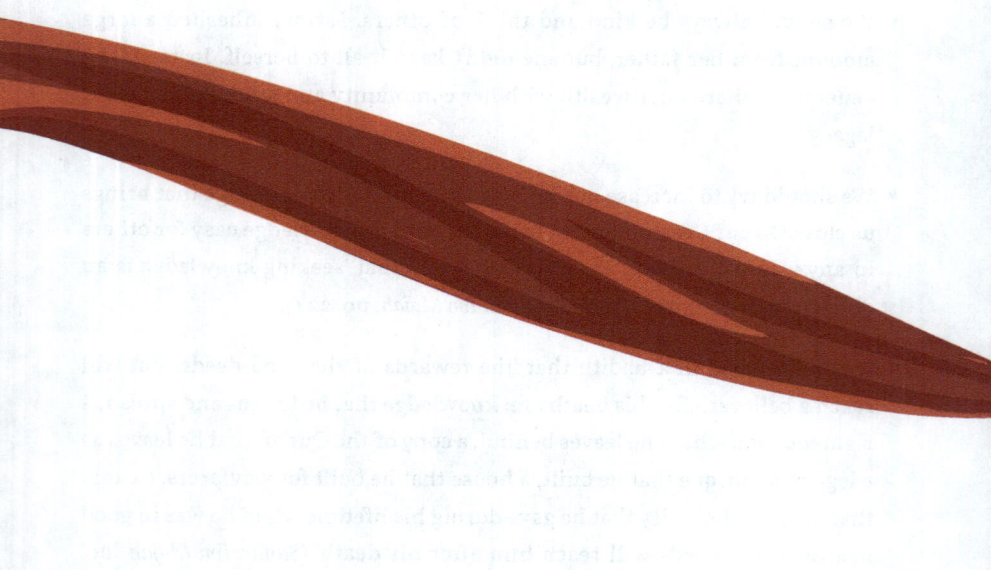

Raziya Sultan

The Only Female Ruler of Delhi
13th century, Delhi Sultanate

Raziya Sultan, also known as Radhiyah bint Iltutmish, was the extraordinary daughter of Shams al-Din Iltutmish. She was born in 1205 CE in the Delhi Sultanate (in modern-day India) and was of Seljuk ancestry. Her father was a former Turkish slave who had risen to power to become the sultan of Delhi due to his competence and exceptional skills. He was an excellent ruler and a forward-thinking person. Raziya's mother, Qutb Begum, was the daughter of Qutb al-Din Aibak, the first sultan of Delhi. She married Iltutmish due to his bravery and brilliance.

Raziya was raised to be courageous and, like her brothers, was given training in administration, statesmanship, governance, and military warfare.

She possessed all the qualities of a strong ruler. Whenever Iltutmish would go on a campaign, he would leave Raziya in charge of the kingdom in his absence, preferring her over her brothers.

Raziya was outspoken and diligently assisted her father in

state affairs. She consistently demonstrated that she was an exemplary leader and capable of governing a kingdom. Unfortunately, Iltutmish's eldest and most capable son, Nasir al-Din Mahmud, died at the age of twenty. Therefore, when Iltutmish was on his deathbed, he appointed his most trusted and competent child, Raziya, as his successor. He believed she was the best person to rule the kingdom and used to say that Raziya was equal to twenty of his sons in ability.

This was the first time a sultan had ever chosen a woman as heir. Although Raziya was highly skilled and competent, this news shocked the Turkish nobles, who found the idea of a woman ruling over them absurd and unbearable. After Iltutmish's death, they rejected Raziya as heir of the kingdom. Instead, they placed her half-brother Rukn al-Din Firuz on the throne, even though he was unfit to be king. Firuz proved to be an incompetent ruler who busied himself with other pursuits, and the people of Delhi were not happy.

Raziya did not want the kingdom to suffer any longer. After a few months of watching the kingdom beginning to crumble, she took action. When he was alive, her father had decreed that anyone who sought justice should do so at the masjid during Friday prayers. In keeping with this tradition, Raziya presented herself before the people in a red robe, the customary colour of one seeking justice. She appealed to the people and to the army, asking for their support in her bid for the throne. She reminded them that their beloved Sultan Iltutmish had appointed her as a successor and assured them she would be a just and and excellent ruler. Convinced by her pleas, they offered Raziya their full support. Finally, Firuz was defeated and executed. The kingdom was finally at peace under Raziya Sultan's protection and leadership.

Raziya claimed her rightful place on the throne under the name Jalalat al-Din Raziya. She was adamant that she be addressed as 'Sultan' and refused to be addressed as 'Sultana', which was typically the title given to the wife of a sultan. She wanted it to be clear that she earned this title on her own merit and was acknowledged justly.

Raziya was crowned and lived in the Turquoise Palace. She ordered coins to be minted in her name – 'Pillar of Women, Queen of the Times, Sultan Raziya, Daughter of Shams al-Din Iltutmish'. Many coins have survived to this day. Raziya was also valiant warrior and commander who led battles and conquered new lands, expanding her kingdom. She rode into battles at the head of her army on a mighty elephant. In addition to achieving military conquests, Raziya established schools, academies and public libraries. From Raziya's reign arose prosperity and justice.

Raziya was criticised for her tolerance and support of an Abyssinian slave named Jamal al-Din Yaqut. She continuously promoted him to higher positions of authority. The nobles were not pleased. They considered Yaqut to be inferior because of his origins. This led to feelings of jealousy and resentment among them, and soon terrible rumours were spread about her, which were never verified. These rumours caused a great deal of grief for Raziya, especially when one of her own childhood friends and current governors, Malik Altunia revolted against her. He defeated her in battle and Raziya was taken prisoner. The nobles took the opportunity to dethrone her and appointed Raziya's brother Muiz al-Din Bahram Shah as their new ruler.

Events took a surprising turn, and Raziya ended up marrying Altunia. After their marriage, they decided to reclaim the kingdom from her brother, and they marched together with their forces towards Delhi. However, they were ultimately defeated, and Raziya never regained her rule.

Raziya Sultan ruled Delhi from 1236 to 1240 CE. She was the first and last female ruler of Delhi. She was a benevolent and just ruler, completely devoted to her kingdom. She promoted all types of education, including learning about the Qur'an and Islam. Raziya loved to mingle with the people in the marketplace to hear and address their grievances. She genuinely cared for her people and was greatly respected and loved by them.

Raziya possessed all the qualities of a great monarch. When power was snatched away from her, she did everything in her capacity to reclaim her position. She was truly an extraordinary woman. The renowned world traveller, Ibn Batuta, mentioned Raziya Sultan in his writings. He reported that 'She ruled as an absolute monarch and mounted a horse like a man, armed with bow and quiver and without veiling her face.'

Reflections

- Even if we face difficulties and opposition from people, we should never stop fighting for justice. We learn about the importance of justice in a hadith Qudsi, 'O My slaves, I have forbidden zulm (injustice, wrongdoing, unfairness) to Myself and I have made it haraam among you, so do not wrong one another.' (*Muslim, no.2577*).

- We should seek support from those around us and use our voices collectively to make a positive difference.

- No matter how humble our beginnings, it's where we end up that counts. Let us believe in ourselves even when others don't. When people say, 'you can't', we should show them that we can by being dedicated and committed to our goals.

- We should not believe or spread rumours. Not only is it sinful, but it can also cause a lot of harm. The rumours may not even be true. They may be a ruse created by an enemy or a jealous person to damage someone's reputation. The Prophet Muhammad ﷺ taught us that 'the Muslim is the one from whose tongue and hands the people are safe, and the believer is the one from whom the people's lives and wealth are safe'. (*Sunan al-Nasa'i, no. 4995*).

- When Raziya needed help, she followed the wisdom of her father and addressed her people directly. She humbled herself, adding a personal touch and demonstrating her sincerity in wanting their support. Sometimes, power lies in having a direct influence on the people on the ground and ultimately turning to Allah ﷻ for help.

Discussion Questions

1. Who was Raziya's greatest supporter?
2. What were the difficulties Raziya experienced during her rule?
3. Have you ever been discriminated against or stereotyped? How did it

REMARKABLE *Muslim Women*

make you feel?

4. Do you think there is a difference between how some cultures treat women and the honour Islam gives them?

5. Give an example of racism in the story.

6. Why do you think people are racist?

Sayyida al-Hurra

A Powerful Governor and Political Genius

15th century, al-Andalus

Sayyida al-Hurra was born around 1485. Her real name is thought to have been Aisha bint Ali ibn Rashid al-Alami. However, she was best known by her title, Sayyida al-Hurra, which means 'free and independent noble lady'. To her critics, however, she was a 'pirate queen'. Her family was from a noble clan that claimed to be descendants of Prophet Muhammad ﷺ.

Sayyida al-Hurra was from the kingdom of Granada, which was the last Muslim-ruled state in Spain. The ancestors of the Muslims of Granada ruled al-Andalus (in modern-day Spain and Portugal) for more than eight hundred years, creating one of the most exquisite civilisations Europe had ever seen. However, this was not to last. In 1491 CE, Abu Abdullah al-Saghir, the last governor in al-Andalus, signed a treaty surrendering Granada in exchange for a guarantee of religious freedom and fair treatment for Muslims. The keys to the kingdom were given to Ferdinand and Isabel, king and queen of Aragon and Castile, in 1492, marking the end of Muslim rule in the Iberian Peninsula.

The new rulers of the monarchy were Christian. Muslim rulers had treated all religious groups under their rule with generosity and respect, but the new Christian rulers were intolerant and despised anyone with different beliefs. They broke their agreement and forced Muslims and Jews to either convert to Christianity or leave their homeland. During this time, more than twenty thousand Muslims were expelled from Spain, and more than a hundred thousand Muslims were murdered by the Spanish armies.

After the fall of Granada, Sayyida al-Hurra and her family fled across the Mediterranean Sea to Morocco as refugees. Her father founded and led the city-state of Chaouen (modern-day Chefchaouen), near Morocco's northern coast, and welcomed other Andalusis fleeing the Spanish Reconquista.

Despite her pleasant childhood, Sayyida never forgot about the trauma her family and other Muslims in al-Andalus experienced when they were forced to leave their beloved homeland. These experiences sparked a burning desire for vengeance.

Sayyida al-Hurra received a first-class education. She studied theology and was fluent in several languages, including Castilian Spanish and Portuguese. One of her teachers was the renowned Moroccan scholar Abdullah al-Ghazwani. Abdullah's equally well-known father is said to have placed his hand on Sayyida al-Hurra's head and stated, 'This girl will rise high in rank.' In 1510, Sayyida al-Hurra married the governor of Titawin (modern-day Tétouan), who was also a refugee many years her senior. Their marriage was marked by mutual respect and affection.

The Titawin estuary was Morocco's major port for trade. Sayyida al-Hurra served as a co-ruler of Titawin, and her brother was made vizier to the sultan of Fez. Her husband had complete trust in her authority and handed her the reins of power each time he was away from the city.

Together with her husband, Aisha fortified the city and built a grand masjid. After her husband's demise, she became the sole ruler of Titawin and took on the title "Sayyida al-Hurra, Hakimat Titwan"—Sovereign Lady, Governor of Titawin.

At the time, Morocco did not have a navy. It depended on privateers to defend the coast. Privateers were people who owned ships and were hired by governments to do jobs. Many of them were Andalusis who had settled in places like Titawin. Sayyida al-Hurra formed an alliance with the privateer Oruc Reis. Oruc was a skilled and fierce warrior who was feared by his enemies. Oruc had a silver prosthetic arm. Despite this, he was extremely strong and fought like a lion.

He had earned the nickname Baba Oruc (Father Oruc), for heroically transporting Muslim refugees from the Iberian Peninsula to North Africa between 1504 and 1510. However, his name was mispronounced as 'Barbarossa' by the Europeans.

Oruc and the other privateers helped Sayyida al-Hurra fight the hostile Iberians who were colonising Morocco and enslaving the population. They became a great threat to the Iberians.

Sayyida al-Hurra's soldiers raided their ships and towns and took Christian captives. She would then demand a ransom from the Spanish and Portuguese in the form of released prisoners. The ransoms she received would be used to help refugees who, like her family, had lost everything when they were driven out of Spain. She rebuilt her city and caused it to flourish.

Sayyida al-Hurra staunchly continued to defend her land from aggressive colonial powers. She became well-known to her enemies by her title, which was included in official documents as 'Sida el-Horra'.

Under her leadership, which lasted for over thirty years, the city achieved unprecedented success and prosperity.

As Sayyida al-Hurra's power and reputation grew, she received a marriage proposal from King Ahmed al-Wattasi. She accepted and insisted that the wedding take place in Titawin. Ahmed did what she asked, and for the first time in Moroccan history, a sultan married outside the capital. Sayyida al-Hurra, who was now also queen, remained governor of Titawin after her marriage. But trouble was on the horizon for Sayyida al-Hurra. Her son-in-law arrived in Titawin in 1542 with a small army and dethroned her. She moved to Chaouen and died twenty years later, in 1561.

Sayyida al-Hurra is considered one of the most important female figures of the Islamic West in the modern age. Her education, bold character, and political genius fuelled her to challenge her enemies, whom she brought to their knees.

Sayyida al-Hurra

Sayyida al-Hurra took strength from her past pain and the suffering of her people. She rebuilt her city and herself. She was a daring naval power, a strategic thinker, and a generous queen. She was expelled from her homeland because of her Muslim faith, but she quickly embraced the new city of Titawin, rebuilding it with her blood, sweat and tears. Today, the old town of Titawin is a UNESCO world heritage site, where Sayyida al-Hurra's legacy lives on. Sayyida al-Hurra was the last Muslim woman ruler to hold the title 'al-Hurra'.

Reflections

- Sayyida al-Hurra did not allow the trauma that she and her family endured to crush her. She worked tirelessly and eventually became a powerful ruler and an excellent political leader.

- Negative experiences can be a motivation to do better and work harder. Sayyida al-Hurra could never return to her first home, but she did everything in her capacity to build a new home. Her vision was to make the city of Titawin safe against enemies.

- Sayyida al-Hurra brought hope to her people as well as new riches. We should not despair in times of hardship but recognise our own self-worth, even when it is denied by others. We all have something to offer.

- Sayidda al-Hurra did not work alone. She joined forces with those who had similar mindsets and values. Reach out and work in collaboration with others to become more impactful in your mission.

- She did not allow herself to be defined by the bad things that happened to her. What was important was who she became and the legacy that she left.

Discussion Questions

1. What do you think of the treatment of Muslims in Spain at the time of Sayyida al-Hurra?

2. Why is it important to learn about Islamic history?

3. What makes Sayyida al-Hurra one of the most powerful women in Islamic history?

4. Do you feel it is fair to blame people for defending their land from enemies and brand them as pirates?

5. Can you think of anyone else in Islamic history who was expelled from their beloved city because of their Muslim faith and made their new city their legacy?

6. Do you think the leaders of today are as good as the leaders of the past? And why?

Nana Asma'u

A Poet, a Scholar and Pioneer in Education
19th century, Sokoto Caliphate

Nana Asma'u was the daughter of Shaykh Usman Dan Fodiyo, the magnificent founder and caliph of the Sokoto Caliphate, one of the most powerful African kingdoms of the nineteenth century. In addition to being of noble lineage and distinctive rank, she was from a family of scholars whose aim was to spread knowledge.

Nana Asma'u and her twin brother Hassan were born in 1793 in the Sokoto Caliphate (in modern-day Nigeria). Although the duo were their father's twenty-second and twenty-third children, he raised them with great care and attention. Asma'u was named after Asma bint Abu Bakr ؓ, the beloved daughter of Abu Bakr al-Siddeeq ؓ. Asma bint Abu Bakr ؓ was a tenacious and resilient woman, and a famous narrator of hadith. 'Nana' is an honorific that means 'lady'. Nana Asma'u's father was a true advocate for education for men, women, and the underprivileged in society. As a child, Nana Asma'u attended one of the local schools founded by her father.

Nana Asma'u received an exceptional education and became

a prolific author. She wrote her first book after becoming a mother. She was knowledgeable in literature from around the world and fluent in four different languages: classical Arabic, Fula, Hausa and Tamacheq. She was a devout Muslim, a hafidha of the Qur'an, a scholar in the Islamic sciences and an expert translator of sacred texts. She spent much of her time in reflection and worship.

To bring stability to the region, her father united the warring states across North Africa into the Sokoto Caliphate. Nana Asma'u's primary concern was the education of women and children. She recognised the value of education and the dire need of women in her community and throughout the region to acquire knowledge about Islam. However, there were many obstacles in her path. The African terrain made it hard for teachers to get to communities in need of education, due to the distance and dangerous routes. There was also a lack of resources, as she had only one copy each of her treasured books.

Nana Asma'u concocted an ingenious plan for women to learn from the comfort of their own homes. She wrote elegies, admonitions, and poetry about the founding principles of the caliphate, so that it would be easy for people to memorise and learn. She then selected women from across the caliphate to act as leaders and teachers. These women were known as *jajis*. Nana Asma'u trained the *jajis*, who learned her poems and then went back to their villages in pairs to teach the women and children. The teachers were crowned with a *malfa* – a hat tied with a red turban that acted as a traditional symbol of office. The women of the villages recognised the *malfa* as a sign that a *jaji* had come to teach them. Incredibly, an entire curriculum was delivered to the students in the form of poetry, predominantly through the spoken word.

Nana Asma'u's educational movement became known as the Yan Taru movement, meaning 'those who congregate' and 'sisterhood'. The students included the most vulnerable women in society, including widows, divorcées, and young girls. The social services provided by the Yan Taru included delivering babies, washing bodies according to Islamic custom, cleaning masjids, providing advice about marital issues, teaching the correct way to perform prayers and teaching children how to read and write Arabic. The journey from one remote village to another was challenging; the *jajis* had to trudge through rainstorms and sandstorms, and were also exposed to predators and poisonous insects. However, their passion and commitment to spreading knowledge kept them steadfast in their pursuit of teaching. The services of the Yan Taru were free of cost, carried out by selfless volunteers.

Gradually, thanks to Nana Asma'u's revolutionary educational system, the communities became empowered with education. They learned about the Qur'an and the Sunnah, personal hygiene, and prophetic medicine. Many superstitious and un-Islamic practices were exposed as ignorant and harmful. *Jajis* still exist today, travelling to educate women across lands using the poems and wisdom of Nana Asma'u.

Nana Asma'u was an invaluable source of counsel to the rulers of the Sokoto Caliphate. For example, she was an adviser to her brother Muhammad Bello when he became caliph. She wrote instructions to governors and debated with the scholars of foreign princes. She maintained correspondence with other female scholars from as far away as Morocco and collected manuscripts from the East, which she would simplify and translate for the benefit of her students.

Nana Asma'u's husband was an important part of her life. She was close to him, and they co-authored books together. He was a grand vizier to the Sokoto Caliphate. She was married to him for about fifty years. When he passed away, she wrote a eulogy for him, in which she did not mention his worldly titles and accomplishments but focused on his human virtue and his generosity.

Nana Asma'u revolutionised education in her community, teaching Islam in an easy-to-remember and easy-to-understand method. She taught according to the ability of her students. She was hard-working and generous with her time. She highly valued education and lived a long, blessed life dedicated to the advancement of others. Nana Asma'u passed away in 1864 and is considered one of the greatest women of the nineteenth century.

Reflections

- Nana Asma'u made learning both easy and convenient. We should think of ways to make things easy for people. The Prophet Muhammad ﷺ said, 'And whoever alleviates the need of a needy person, Allah will alleviate his needs in this world and the hereafter' (*Sahih Muslim*, no.36).

- Nana Asma'u was a devout Muslim who understood the importance Islam places on attaining knowledge for every woman and man. The Prophet Muhammad ﷺ said, 'And whoever follows a path to seek knowledge therein, Allah will make easy for him a path to Paradise' (*Sahih Muslim*, no. 1508).

- She was kind enough to use her power and influence to empower women and children in her society. We should use our talents and abilities and whatever influence we have to benefit others, especially those who are underprivileged. This can be done by providing a service, establishing a mentorship relationship, or setting up a beneficial programme.

- Nana Asma'u's intention was purely for the sake of Allah ﷻ and for Islam. We should purify our intentions regularly, so that our work can be blessed and accepted. We learn in a hadith that actions are by their intentions. The Prophet ﷺ said, 'He who lets the people hear of his good deeds intentionally to win their praise, Allah will let the people know his real intention [on the Day of Resurrection], and he who does good things in public to show off and win the praise of the people, Allah will disclose his real intention [and humiliate him]' (*Sahih al-Bukhari*, no. 6499).

Discussion Questions

1. What did Nana Asma'u do to overcome the obstacles that got in the way of teaching underprivileged communities?

2. What was the role of a *jaji*?

3. Why is education vital?

REMARKABLE *Muslim Women*

4. Does everyone learn in the same way?

5. Which do you think is most important: a person's qualifications or the way they make someone else feel?

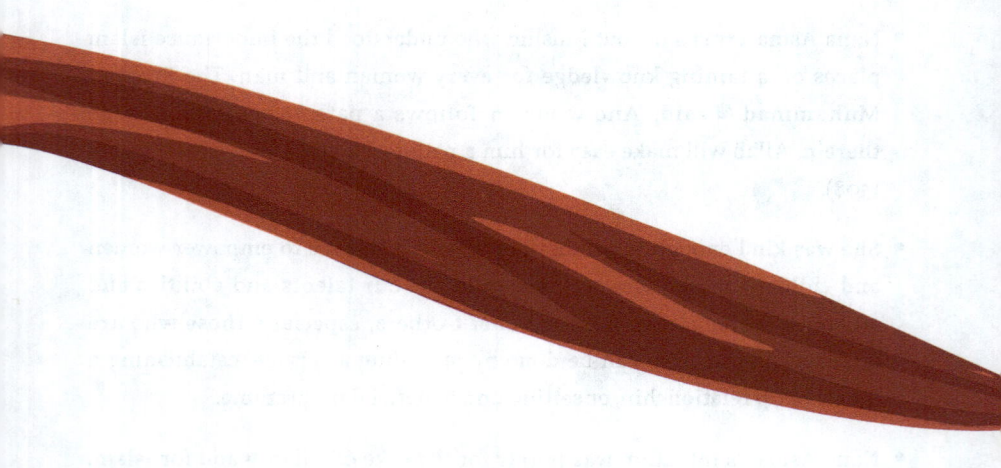

Cut Nyak Dhien

A Guerriila Commander and National Hero
19th century, Aceh Sultanate, Sumatra Island

Cut Nyak Dhien (also known as Tjut Nyak Dien) was born in 1848 into Acehnese nobility (in modern-day Indonesia). Her family was part of the Muslim Acehnese aristocracy. Her father was a chieftain. Cut Nyak Dhien was educated in both household matters and in Islam. She was renowned for her beauty, and men raced to propose to her. Her parents arranged her marriage whilst she was quite young to Teuku Ibrahim Lamnga, who was also the son of a chief from a noble family.

In 1873, the Dutch invaded and proclaimed war, beginning the Aceh War. During this time, both Cut Nyak Dhien's husband and father fought valiantly to defend their land against the Dutch invaders through the Sultan's guerrilla war against the Dutch. Cut Nyak Dhien's husband and father eventually lost their lives when they were ambushed by the Dutch in a battle known as the Battle of Sela Glee Tarun. Upon hearing the news, Cut Nyak Dhien promised to take revenge against the Dutch colonisers.

Cut Nyak Dhien started leading guerrilla units in the war against the Dutch until she united her forces with those of guerrilla leader Teuku Umar. Impressed by her piety and her assertion that her father and husband should not be mourned because they had been martyred and entered heaven, Umar proposed to her. They soon married, and she became his chief strategist and political mentor. The union boosted the morale of the Aceh armies. The couple gave birth to a daughter, whom they named Cut Gambang.

The war with the Dutch continued, and Teuku Umar and Cut Nyak Dhien made a strategic move to surrender to the Dutch forces. In the belief that they had switched sides, and impressed by their knowledge and skillset, the Dutch army appointed Umar as a commander in chief of a Dutch army unit. However, years later, when the Dutch thought Umar and Cut Nyak Dhien set out to attack Aceh loaded with warfare equipment, weapons, and ammunition, it was discovered that their intention was to support the Acehnese using these resources. All these years later, their loyalty remained with their people.

Cut Nyak Dhien and her husband continued the triumphant resistance against the Dutch with their powerful new weaponry. Unfortunately, when the Dutch sent military police troops, Cut Nyak Dhien and her army were unable to defeat them. Many Acehnese were killed by the Dutch forces, including innocent men, women, and children. The Dutch launched a surprise attack on Teuku Umar, killing him during battle in 1899. When Cut

Gambang wept over her father's death, Cut Nyak Dhien strengthened her daughter by telling her, 'As Acehnese women, we must not shed tears for anyone who becomes a martyr.' She kept these words in mind even as she grieved the loss of her husband.

Even after the death of her second husband, Cut Nyak Dhien did not give up the fight. She took control of the guerrilla army and persisted against the Dutch. Inevitably, due to old age, her health declined. Suffering from blindness and arthritis, she retreated with her army further into the jungle. The number of her troops fell dramatically, and they lacked military resources. On the condition that she be treated fairly, one of her men, Pang Laot, informed the Dutch about the secret location of her headquarters. They were shocked by the arrival of the Dutch army. Despite fiercely fighting back, she was captured. Fortunately, her brave daughter, Cut Gambang, escaped deep into the jungle and continued the resistance, following in the footsteps of her heroic parents.

The Dutch exiled Cut Nyak Dhien to West Java because they feared she would resurrect the Aceh resistance. She taught the Qur'an and was eventually nicknamed Dhien Ibu Perbu (Dhien the Queen) by the locals. Her knowledge of Islamic Arabic texts and piety impressed even prominent Islamic leaders. She died in November 1908 and was proclaimed a national heroine by President Sukrano, the first president of Indonesia, in May 1964. The Cut Nyak Dhien Airport in Aceh is named in her honour.

Her image has been featured on Indonesian stamps and banknotes, and a 1988 film about her life – Tjoet Nja' Dhien – won awards.

Cut Nyak Dhien, a devout Muslimah, an Acehnese strategist, and a freedom fighter who possessed an unbreakable spirit. Despite having been widowed twice, and losing the war, she did not give up on life. When she was exiled and appeared to lose everything she had once known, including her prestige, her family and her beloved home, she did not fall into despair. Instead, she rebuilt her life once again by holding tightly to the Qur'an and teaching it to others. She continued to benefit her community even in the final stages of her life. She is not only an Indonesian national hero, but an example of resistance and courage to the entire world.

Reflections

- In the face of adversity and continuous trials and hardship, we should not give up. We should be resilient, just like Cut Nyak Dhien.

- More than our appearance, it is our piety and connection to Allah that truly matters.

- Joining forces with others who are doing good work will enable us to be even more successful together.

- We should not work for applause but for a good cause. Years after her death, Cut Nyak Dhien was proclaimed a national hero. We may not see the fruits of our labour today, but our legacy will live on – either quietly or celebrated in history – long after we have left this world. Our good deeds and good intentions are what truly hold weight.

- This verse from the Qur'an – 'God is the Lord of those who believe; He brings them out of darkness and into light' (Qur'an, Surah al-Baqarah, 2:257) – beautifully encapsulates Cut Nyak Dhien's story. Even though she had great loss and darkness in her life, Allah ﷻ gave her life meaning again and brought the light of the Qur'an and a blessed purpose back into her life.

Discussion Questions

1. How can challenges make a person stronger?

2. What makes a good leader?

3. What does patience look like? Does it mean doing nothing, or does it mean using any means necessary to improve our situation without losing faith?

4. What was Cut Nyak's Dhien's ultimate strength: her beauty or her faith?

Lady Evelyn Cobbold

The First British-Born Woman to Perform Hajj

19th century, Scotland

Lady Evelyn Cobbold, also known as Lady Zainab Cobbold, considered herself to be a Muslim from as far back as she could remember. Even though she was not born into a Muslim home and had not been raised as a Muslim, she had always felt that she was Muslim at heart.

Lady Evelyn was born in Edinburgh in 1867. She was the eldest daughter of the Scottish peer and explorer Charles Adolphus Murray, seventh Earl of Dunmore. Her mother, Lady Gertrude Coke, was the daughter of the second Earl of Leicester. Lady Evelyn's father had an intense love for the Scottish moors and mountains and a passion for travelling. Lady Evelyn was influenced by her father and was proud of her Scottish roots.

Lady Evelyn was an inspirational woman of many talents: an adventurous traveller, author, expert deerstalker and first-class angler (fisher). As a Scottish aristocrat and Mayfair socialite, she was the owner of a beautiful estate in the Scottish Highlands and a breath-taking deer forest in Glencarron.

Since childhood, Lady Evelyn had been surrounded by

Muslims. She spent most of her childhood in Algiers and Cairo, as her father loved to travel during the winter months to these warmer Muslim lands. There, Evelyn learned to speak Arabic and grew familiar with the Muslim way of life and Islamic traditions. Her favourite thing to do was escape her governess and visit the masjids with her Algerian friends, 'unconsciously becoming a little Muslim at heart', as she put it.

Years later, when Lady Evelyn happened to be in Rome, she met the Pope. He asked her if she was a Catholic. Lady Evelyn did not expect this question and was taken aback for a moment, but then proudly replied that she was a Muslim.

Lady Evelyn had not thought about Islam for many years, but after her declaration to the Pope, she felt a sudden determination to study it. The more she read about Islam, the more convinced she became that it was the most practical religion. She thought of it as the religion of common sense and believed it could solve the world's many complicated problems and bring peace and happiness to humanity.

In 1929, at the age of sixty-two, Lady Evelyn started making plans for the most important journey of her life: the pilgrimage to Makkah. Every Muslim is required to do Hajj at least once in their life if they have the means to do so. Muslims from all over the world, of different races, from different countries, speaking different languages and from different backgrounds, all gather once a year for this blessed rite.

Once Lady Evelyn made the intention to perform hajj, she

contacted Saudi Arabia's minister in London to inform him of her desire to visit the Holy City. The minister then wrote a letter to the King of Saudi Arabia to request formal permission for Lady Evelyn to go to Makkah. She did everything in her power to ensure that her request was not declined, using influential people in her social circle to help accomplish her goal. She anxiously awaited the king's reply. At last, at the age of sixty-five, Lady Evelyn's great wish was to be fulfilled. She was finally granted special permission by the King of Saudi Arabia to perform the sacred pilgrimage.

Entering the Great Masjid of Makkah for the first time, Lady Evelyn was amazed. She had never imagined anything more astonishing. She described the hajj as 'one of the most soul-inspiring experiences that has ever been granted to human beings.' As the first British-born woman on record to perform the blessed Muslim pilgrimage in the Holy City of Makkah, she became a celebrity.

In 1934, she wrote a heartfelt description of her unforgettable journey in her book, *Pilgrimage to Mecca*. She said,

> When I look into my Journal, I shall live it all again. Time cannot rob me of the memories that I treasure in my heart, the gardens of Medina, the peace of its Mosques, the countless pilgrims who passed me with shining eyes of faith, the wonder and glory of the Haram of Mecca, the Great Pilgrimage through the desert and the hills to Arafaat, and above all the abiding sense of joy and

fulfilment that possesses the soul. What have the past days held out but endless interest, wonder and beauty? To me an amazing new world has been revealed. [1]

Lady Evelyn's pilgrimage and her book received a great deal of media attention. The British press wrote positively about Lady Evelyn's amazing journey to Makkah, as it was a great but rare achievement for that time.

Lady Evelyn died in 1963 on a bitter cold day, at the age of ninety-six. She loved nature and was buried, just as she had requested, on a distant hillside on her Glencarron estate, Wester Ross, in the Scottish Highlands. Even though Lady Evelyn had lost contact with other Muslims over the years, she had remained true to her faith until the very end of her life. She made sure that she would have a Muslim burial by leaving special written instructions for her funeral. Lady Evelyn clearly requested that the verse 'Allah ﷻ is the Light of the heavens and the earth' be inscribed on a flat slab and placed on her grave (Qur'an, Surah al-Nur, 24:35).

Since no imams were known in Scotland at that time, one travelled from afar just to perform the burial rites for the funeral, as well as the prayers Lady Evelyn had requested. Just as she wished, a piper played laments while Surah al-Nur was recited in Arabic.

---

[1] Cobbold, Lady Evelyn. Pilgrimage to Mecca. London: Arabian Publishing, 1934.

Lady Evelyn Cobbold

Lady Evelyn's contribution to Hajj travel literature and her place as a pioneering female traveller should be celebrated and not forgotten. She accomplished an extraordinary collection of firsts. She was the first British woman on record to perform the hajj. She was also the first foreign pilgrim outside King 'Abd al-'Aziz ibn Saud's court to make the pilgrimage by car, and the first person to ride the new pilgrim buses introduced in 1933. In addition, she claimed to be the first woman to travel by air to Africa, on a flying-boat, in 1935.

Lady Evelyn was an extraordinary British Muslimah. She was able to do something no British traveller before her had been able to: describe the private female side of domestic life in Makkah and Madinah. This and her religious commitment set her journey and book apart from previous English descriptions of the Hejaz. It is indeed a great legacy to leave behind.

Reflections

- Without action, there is no gain. Lady Evelyn long wished to perform hajj, so she took the necessary steps to acquire special permission to go on the blessed pilgrimage.

- Be passionate and seek to educate others. Lady Evelyn wrote a detailed book in the form of a diary about her experiences and travels to Makkah. She understood it was up to her to share her experience with the world and

REMARKABLE

provide a true account of her journey. She wanted to dispel any false opinions British people had about the people of Makkah.

- Lady Evelyn had the honour of staying in Makkah as a guest and mixing with the people. She enjoyed the rare opportunity to see and experience first-hand the peaceful and happy way people lived.

- Be brave. Lady Evelyn was a well-educated Muslim who understood the beauty of Islam. She was courageous enough to proudly tell the Pope that she was a Muslim.

- Faith can be something private between a person and Allah. To be a Muslim, one doesn't have to disclose their faith to others or have witnesses. All they have to do is say the shahadah sincerely with their heart and tongue, preferably in Arabic and also in their mother tongue.

Discussion Questions

1. What talents did Lady Evelyn have? What are your talents?
2. Do you think it's easy to speak the truth, or does it require courage?
3. How did Lady Evelyn describe Islam?
4. What do you think are some of the difficulties converts experience?
5. Can you think of ways to welcome and provide support to new Muslims?
6. Does the media report on Islam and Muslims accurately? Do you think this is done on purpose? If so, why?

Şule Yüksel Şenler

A Writer and Hijab Activist
20th century, Turkey

Ş ule Yüksel Şenler was born in 1938 in Kayseri, Turkey to a secular family. The family later settled in Istanbul. Şule had to drop out of school in the eighth grade and started work when her family went bankrupt, and her mother became ill. She worked as an assistant to a tailor, but later discovered her true calling as a writer. When she was just fourteen years old, Şule's stories were published in *Yelpaze* magazine, and later she began writing articles for *Kadın* ('Woman') newspaper. She went on to become a successful writer, journalist, and hijab activist, although she initially had no interest in wearing the hijab.

Turkey at that time promoted secularism, which meant that the state regulated religion and did not allow Muslims to practise their faith publicly. Muslim women had to appear less Muslim and downplay their religious views or be at risk of criticism or discrimination. Because the Turkish government prohibited headscarves for women working in the public sector, women had to make the choice between wearing hijab or pursuing education and professional careers.

In her twenties, Şule became interested in the work of Said Nursi, who was a Muslim theologian who played an important role in the revival of Islam in Turkey. Şule started attending the meetings of Nursi's followers. However, she still had no desire to wear the hijab. When questioned at meetings about her clothes, she declared, 'If you don't accept me like this, I won't come again.' Her opinion would later change completely, and the hijab would play a significant part in the rest of her life.

Şule's brother Özer was unlike the rest of his family. He was a follower of Nursi and played a key role in Şule's transformation. Özer advised her to read *Risale-i Nur*, a popular book by Nursi. The book struck a chord with her and gave her a new perspective. In 1965, at the age of twenty-seven, Şule proudly embraced all parts of her faith. She bloomed into a strong and empowered woman dedicated to her faith. She began to pray and unapologetically wear the hijab. She finally united her outer appearance with the strong religious beliefs in her heart.

Şule was a pioneer as the first veiled journalist in Turkey. She used her platform to write articles about Muslim women and the hijab. In addition, she published a magazine with her brother to promote hijabs and modest clothing for Muslim women. In the 1960s and 1970s, her articles and revolutionary speeches throughout Turkey empowered young women to embrace their Islamic identity and wear the hijab to school. Whilst prominent newspapers were calling the headscarf 'the pain in Turkey's head', Şule criticised the hijab ban publicly and worked to empower faithful, practising Muslim women.

Şule herself became a ground-breaking designer in modest fashion. Her designs were met with overwhelming success and popularity. Şule's influence was powerful. Women who donned the hijab in her style were called Şulebaş, or 'Şule heads'. She became one of the most renowned names in the struggle of Muslim women for religious freedom and a leading figure in the revival of the hijab.

Şule's activism did not go unopposed. She faced a barrage of lawsuits, including one in 1967 by the Turkish Women's Union for an article in which she wrote, 'It is a must that Muslim women put on their headscarves.'

Şule's activism became a threat to the secular authorities and to everyone who opposed her message of religious freedom. They could not tolerate a woman in a hijab having so much power and influence. The then-president of Turkey, Cevdet Sunay, declared in 1971: 'Those behind (the increasing number of) covered women on the streets will be punished.'

In response to the president's threat, the brave Şule wrote a letter demanding that he 'should apologise to Allah ﷻ and the nation'. Consequently, Şule was charged with insulting the president and jailed for eight months. After a public outcry in support of Şule, the president issued a pardon two months into her sentence. However, Şule refused the pardon and served the full term, despite her ill health. After she was released from prison, she defiantly continued her activism via lectures, articles and books for many years and worked as a journalist for several newspapers up until the early 2000s.

Şule was a bestselling author. Her books include *Woman in Islam and Today*, *Tears of the Civilization*, *The Girl and the Flower and Suffering of the Youth*, *What Happened to Us?* Her bestselling book *Peace Street* was adapted into a popular film, *Crossroads*, in 1979 and into a TV series under the book's original title in 2012.

Şule took her last breath on 28 August 2019 and passed away at eighty-one years of age. President Recep Tayyip Erdoğan issued a condolence message on Twitter, accompanied by a photo of himself with Şule. President Erdoğan, along with hundreds of women wearing the hijab, attended the funeral prayers for the remarkable Şule Yüksel Şenler, who had dedicated her life to the rights of practising Muslim women and religious freedom.

Şule was a true pioneer in more ways than one. She remained strong in her struggle to support women's God-given right to wear the hijab. As a modest fashion designer, she catered specifically to the needs of Muslim women. She was an activist dedicated to improving the status of Muslim women in Turkish society. Şule did not cower in the face of power and was prepared to go to prison, all to free Muslim women from the oppression of those who wanted to control their dresscode. She was a great reformer, a writer, an instigator of change, a powerful role model and an inspiration to the youth and the underrepresented. She remains an incredible inspiration today.

Reflections

- While it's popular to say that a woman should be free to wear what she wants to wear, the hijab of a Muslim woman is still debated. This is an obvious double standard. In some parts of the world, women can dress as they like, covering as much or as little as they want, unless they are practising Muslim women. In such cases, their rights are curtailed, and their choice is belittled.

- Although Şule only embraced wearing the hijab at a later stage in her life (age twenty-seven), this did not deter her from becoming a hijab activist. Once she realised the importance of the hijab for a Muslim woman, she recognised their right to religious freedom and did not fear the taunts of people who judged her for her past. Like Şule, we shouldn't let our past actions define our future. When we learn something of benefit, we should spread it and not be afraid of being judged. Şule became the reason that generations of Muslim women had the strength to embrace hijab when secularism was strongly enforced.

- No job is too insignificant. The experience of working as a tailor's assistant gave Şule the tools she would eventually need to design a new headscarf for practising women. There is something to learn in every experience. Use the experience, no matter how little, to do something good and to help others.

- Change takes time. Rally support for a worthwhile cause. We should not allow powerful voices to overshadow ours.

- Standing up for what we know to be right can be scary but living our life without fulfilling our true purpose (obeying Allah) is even scarier. We must trust in Allah and draw our strength from Him. In a world where power is everything, we must remember that Allah is al-Azeez (the Almighty) and al-Qadeer (the Powerful).

- Women in Turkey were persecuted for wearing the hijab and banned from universities. Sadly, this is still the case today. In India, some schools have banned female students from wearing hijab. Muskan Khan, a Muslim student wearing a burqa, was surrounded by men from a far-right Hindu mob who demanded she remove her burqa if she wanted to study. In response, the remarkable Muskan Khan stood tall and remembered Allah, proudly shouting out 'Allahu akbar!' (God is the greatest), before marching on. Just like Şule, she is a powerful inspiration to Muslims everywhere.

Discussion Questions

1. How were Muslim women discriminated against in secular Turkey?

2. Do you think Muslim women are pressured to downplay their religious views even today?

3. Why do Muslim women wear the hijab?

4. *The western media and some individuals tend to comment negatively on the way Muslim women choose to dress and some countries that banned the burqa (face covering and/or hijab) had no problem with people wearing face masks during the Covid-19 pandemic. Perhaps the reason people want to control the way a Muslim women dresses is because they do not like her commitment to Allah, and because she has freedom and power in herself through rejecting what is 'normal'.* Would you agree with this statement?

5. Frantz Fanon said, 'This woman, who sees without being seen, frustrates the colonizer.' What do you think this means?

Zainab al-Ghazali

A Champion of Muslim Women's Rights and Symbol of Resistance

20th century, Egypt

Zainab al-Ghazali was born in Egypt in the year 1917. Her father was a local religious leader and a graduate of the prestigious Al-Azhar University. Even while she was a child, he encouraged Zainab to pursue a leadership role within the community. He urged her to draw inspiration from Nusayba bint Ka'ab ﷺ, a strong and resilient companion of the Prophet ﷺ, who soon became young Zainab's role model.

With a clear vision for success, Zainab became academically qualified in the fields of hadith, dawah and tafsir. Zainab found liberty in her religion. In her quest to be a beneficial member of her community, she joined the Egyptian Feminist Union at the age of sixteen. However, she soon realised that although this organisation focused its work on gender issues and equal rights, it did so from a secular viewpoint and a Western liberal perspective that was incompatible with her moral values. Through her studies of Islam, she knew that women could find what they were searching for in Islam. She renounced her membership of the Egyptian Feminist Union.

At eighteen, she started her own organisation based on Islamic principles. It was known as the Muslim Women's Association, or *Jamaa'at al-Sayyidaat al-Muslimaat*. The organisation's objectives were to educate women and to provide charitable services. Zainab believed that Islam gave women rights that were not granted by any other society. She believed that empowerment, true liberation, and the economic and political rights of women were embedded in the Qur'an. She valued women's contributions at home and within the community. Zainab understood the vital role women play in the world and believed that it was of the utmost importance that Muslim women study Islam so that they understand their rights.

Zainab gave weekly talks at Ibn Tulun Masjid to crowds of three to five thousand people. The MWA garnered an astounding membership of over three million women throughout the country. She regularly taught students at her house, and her husband supported her completely.

Zainab also used her influence and power to give back to the community. She established and maintained orphanages; instituted educational, social reform and development programmes; and helped disadvantaged families and the poor. She arranged mediation for family disputes and started programs to help orphans and widows. Zainab's activism was focused on the betterment of the family unit and of society, the foundation of which was Islam. She found this cause far more empowering and liberating for Muslim women in society than

Zainab al-Ghazali

secular feminism. She concluded that 'Islam gave women rights in the family, granted by no other society'. Amongst other things, she was a writer and editor for the al-Da'wah magazine.

Because Zainab was completely dedicated to her cause of establishing women's rights, she wanted to ensure that nothing came in the way of her activism. When she got married a second time, she included a conditional clause in her marriage contract:

> If that day comes in when a clash is apparent between your personal interests and economic activities on the one hand, and my Islamic work on the other, and that I find my married life is standing in the way of Da'wah and the establishment of an Islamic governing body, then, each of us should go our own way. I cannot ask you today to share with me this struggle, but it is my right on you not to stop me from my struggle in the way of Allah. Moreover, you should not ask me about my activities with other activists, and let trust be full between us. A full trust between a man and a woman, a woman who, at the age of 18, gave her full life to Allah and that of Da'wah. In the event of any clash between the marriage contract's interest and that of Da'wah, our marriage will end, but Da'wah will always remain rooted in me. [2]

It was important for Zainab to be fair and to tell her fiancé about her values and expectations. She wanted to let him know

---

[a] Begg, Moazzam. "The Tortured Scholar | Zaynab al-Ghazali." Islam21C. January 27, 2021.

what he was in for and gave him the opportunity to understand this before the actual marriage took place. She made it clear that her first love was dawah and her commitment to Allah ﷻ and that it would always be that way. It was important for her to be open and honest, as a healthy marriage is based on trust, understanding and mutual respect.

Egypt was going through serious political turbulence. Activists and leaders were arrested and jailed for their resistance against corruption and oppression. The government was suspicious of groups like the Muslim Women's Association. They felt threatened by their influence and power and saw them as rivals, especially since Zainab frequently voiced her concern about political injustices. The government wanted Zainab to endorse them to her followers, and even offered her money and status. However, she refused their offers and remained true to her cause. As a result, Zainab became a target of the government, and assassination attempts were made on her life.

In 1965, the government shut down the Muslim Women's Association and arrested Zainab. She was nearly fifty years old when she was sentenced to a twenty-five-year imprisonment. Many believe that this sentence was based on fabricated conspiracies. Horrifically, Zainab was subjected to indescribable torture in prison. However, her faith helped her to remain resistant and steadfast throughout the immense hardship she faced. Zainab had memorised many verses of the Qur'an and often quoted them in response to the interrogators who were torturing her.

Zainab al-Ghazali

She would make powerful and sincere du'a throughout her time in prison. All these things kept her resolve strong and helped her cope during the most horrendous time of her life.

During this time, Zainab was blessed to experience miracles and have beautiful dreams. One day, after being tortured, she fell asleep whilst still in prostration, her words of remembrance and praise of Allah ﷻ echoing under her breath. She saw the Prophet Muhammad ﷺ in a dream and awoke feeling consoled by his words. She interpreted this to be a reaffirmation that she was on the true path.

When the president of Egypt died, Zainab was finally pardoned and freed. Despite the persecution she suffered, her faith never wavered. In fact, her faith and trust in Allah ﷻ only grew stronger. Soon after she was released from prison, Zainab resumed her activism. She wrote books and articles, including a memoir recounting her gruesome time in jail, *Ayyam min ḥayati* ('Days from my Life'), which was translated into English and published as *Return of the Pharaoh*.

Zainab returned to her Creator in 2005 at the age of 88. She remained at the forefront of empowering Muslim women through the rights given to them by Islam. Following in the footsteps of great female companions like Nusayba ؓ, she remained committed to her faith. She is a great Muslim role model, a leader and a symbol of resistance and strength for every woman and man.

Reflections

- A Muslim woman's empowerment comes from Islam. Zainab al-Ghazali recognised this. She knew that a Muslim woman would only find true liberation in her religion, which is why she campaigned for better Islamic education of women. She was a champion for Muslim women and recognised their crucial role in society.

- Many societies undermine the role of a mother in the family unit. However, Zainab recognised the importance of a woman's role both in the family and in society. She knew that building a stable and strong family leads to a more nurtured and functional society.

- Zainab ensured that her husband understood that her activism came before everything else. In Islam, a woman is allowed to put conditions in her marriage contract, and Zainab wisely used this right given to her by Islam.

- While many women sought fulfilment through secular feminism, Zainab believed that this success could be achieved from Islam without harming the family and disobeying Allah ﷻ. We should continue to gain Islamic knowledge and realise that Islam is a complete way of life, which no ideology or movement can match. We should be careful of movements that try to cause harmful divisions between men and women. The following verse from the Qur'an sums up eloquently the relationship between men and women in Islam: 'The Believers, men and women, are protectors one of another: they enjoin what is just and forbid what is evil: they observe regular prayers, practise regular charity, and obey Allah and His Messenger. On them will Allah pour His mercy: for Allah is Exalted in power, Wise' (Qur'an, Surah al-Tawbah, 9:71).

- We are more than just people who were born to work. We are whole human beings, and the rights that Islam has given us as women (when the conditions are right) allow us to focus on the important things in life, like family, community, and spiritual growth, which you cannot put a price on.

Zainab al-Ghazali

Discussion Questions

1. If someone cares about the rights of women and supports justice, do they automatically become a feminist?

2. Is it fair to credit feminism on the advancement of women?

3. Why did Zainab renounce her membership and withdraw her support from the Egyptian Feminist Union?

4. What is a marriage contract and what is the benefit of having one?

5. What gave Zainab patience and reassurance whilst she was suffering in prison?

Rebiya Kadeer

A Uyghur Activist and Business Mogul
20th century, East Turkestan

Rebiya Kadeer was born in 1946 in Altay, East Turkestan (now Xinjiang, China) to a poor family. The people from her land are known as Uyghurs: a central Asian people who are distant relatives of the Turks. They are a Muslim minority who live in north-western China – a region that Uyghurs call East Turkestan and the Chinese Communist Party (CCP) calls Xinjiang, which means 'the new frontier'.

As a child, Rebiya was captivated by the beauty of her homeland. She was surrounded by lush green forests filled with the sound of birdsong and majestic mountains above which magnificent eagles soared. She was in awe of the peaceful natural environment and the wonderful people at her school and in her neighbourhood. Alas, this was not to last. One day, some Chinese people arrived in her town. This was the first time that Rebiya had laid eyes on a Chinese person. They seemed to be generous and helpful. They swept the streets, wiped windows, and treated the sick. Rebiya and her people were impressed by these new visitors and considered them thoughtful and kind, but things soon changed when their true motives were revealed. These people were working for the Chinese government. They forced the Uyghurs out of their homes and occupied their land.

The lives of Rebiya and of the Uyghur people were shattered and their neighbourhoods destroyed. The Chinese army took over East Turkestan, and the Uyghurs were banished from their own land. Rebiya and her family were put on a huge black truck and sent away. Rebiya, a young child at the time, was deeply wounded by this tragic experience. Her home, her friends, her neighbours – everything that she had ever known and loved – was suddenly snatched away from her and her beloved Uyghur people.

Rebiya grew up in a large family blessed with the presence of orphans her father met during his travels. Unconcerned about whether they were siblings by birth or adoption, all the brothers and sisters formed a strong bond of love. From this experience, Rebiya learnt the true meaning of sacrifice and of what it means to love for others what you love for yourself.

When Rebiya was a little girl, her beloved father would tell her and her siblings a special story about an ant and a bird. The bird, proud of its wings, pitied the small ant. But the ant had a positive mindset and was determined to overcome any obstacle and reach his goal. Many years later, the two met. The bird learned that the ant, despite his size and weak appearance, has triumphed due to his determination and will. The bird had wings, but the ant had willpower, confidence, and hope.

Rebiya Kadeer

The story inspired Rebiya and remained with her for the rest of her life. It taught her that no hurdle was unbeatable, and no goal was too big.

In the 1960s, her family went through even more testing times. They were poor. Rebiya was still a young girl and passionate about attending school. However, she made the ultimate sacrifice for her family. She married a man who had taken pity on them and offered them accommodation. Sadly, she had to give up her greatest love – her schooling and education — so that she could save her family from starvation. Rebiya was married to him for thirteen years and gave birth to six children, but the marriage ended in divorce. For a time, she was separated from her six children, whom she loved very much. She considered this the second most tragic experience of her life. Rebiya found it was hard to survive in her society without the support of a man. She didn't have a job but was determined to make a living and provide a better lifestyle for her children, as their father didn't earn much. She knew that she had to find a way to help them.

Rebiya realised she had two options – either find a job or start a business. Both options would prove to be challenging, because the society in which she lived didn't like the idea of women doing business in the streets on their own.

Rebiya was under tremendous pressure. She initially started doing laundry for people whilst covering her face. Gradually, Rebiya managed to expand her business and, through hard work and excellent character, persuaded people to give her a chance.

She opened a laundry business out of her new home. The business thrived, and several months later, she closed the business and invested some of her earnings into trading commodities.

Rebiya was a brilliant entrepreneur and remarkably successful in her business. She continued to develop her trading enterprise, and in the 1980s, she expanded her interests into real estate. In 1987, she opened a women's bazaar in Ürümqi and followed it with a department store and an accompanying apartment complex in the 1990s. Soon, she expanded her operations to include subsidiaries throughout Central Asia.

From rags to riches, by 1993, Rebiya had become the wealthiest woman in China. Just like the story of the ant she heard many times in her childhood, Rebiya was triumphant. She was praised by the Chinese government as an example of Uyghur success and was appointed to influential organisations and committees, including the Chinese People's Political Consultative Conference and the National People's Congress. In 1995, she served as a delegate to the United Nations Conference on Women, held in Beijing.

During this time, as she pursued her business accomplishments, Rebiya thought long and hard about the oppression of the Uyghur people. They were banished, imprisoned, tortured, and murdered despite being educated and God-fearing people. She questioned why they had to live like this and what she could do to change it. As she thought more deeply about the situation, she realised that she wanted to marry a man who would join her

revolutionary cause. Rebiya knew she had influence, but she needed a heroic figure by her side to support her in her mission to help her people.

In 1981, Rebiya married for the second time. She initially had not wanted to remarry but realised that she needed support in order to pursue both her businesses and ambitions. She found a man who matched her vision in Sidik Haji Rouzi, a professor, poet, and political dissident. He was an intellectual and activist who had been jailed for leading a Uyghur resistance movement against the Chinese authorities in the late 1960s. Rebiya told her new husband that her ultimate goal was to liberate her homeland. They moved to Ürümqi, the capital of Xinjiang, and had five children together. Her husband was later exiled to the United States and began to work there as a pro-East Turkestan independence broadcaster.

With the concern of her people at heart, Rebiya invested in the Uyghur people. She mentored them and created jobs. She established a school on the fifth floor of her department store in Ürümqi, ran literacy programs and opened foreign language schools in Kashgar, Hotan and Aksu. Rebiya was also the driving force behind a charity called the 1,000 Families Mothers' Project, which helped Uyghur women start their own businesses.

Rebiya also became a political activist. Whenever she met with Chinese officials, she took the opportunity to speak about the difficulties experienced by Uyghurs and to raise awareness for human rights' violations against her people. The government did not like this. They stripped her of her government-issued appointments and confiscated her passport. They became suspicious of her, and, in August 1999, she was arrested. She was accused of betraying state secrets and in 2000, she was convicted and sentenced to jail. Thanks to pressure from the international community, her sentence was reduced, and she was released from prison in 2005.

In prison, she witnessed the brutal torture and killing of young Uyghurs. She spent two years in a dark room with no light. She was prohibited from speaking with or seeing other people for the entire time that she was in prison. During her incarceration, Rebiya was warned that if she continued to work for her people, then her wealth would be confiscated, and her family would be punished. Even as she remained in prison, Rebiya was honoured by several international organisations. In 2004, she received the Rafto Prize for Human Rights by Norway and was nominated for the Nobel Peace Prize in 2006.

Despite her imprisonment, nothing was going to stop her from fighting for the rights of her people. Rebiya knew her people needed a leader and a voice to speak up for them. She was not going to abandon them at any cost. The Chinese government threatened and arrested her children and put other family members under surveillance and house arrest. Despite her devastating family situation, Rebiya continued to devote her life to her people's cause. She understood sacrifice at a young age and learned to love for others what she loved for herself.

Rebiya Kadeer

Eventually, Rebiya was exiled to the United States after her release from prison. There, she continued her activism for human rights and Uyghur self-determination.

Rebiya believes that one of the main objectives of the atheist Chinese government is to root out Islam. She says that the authorities have prevented the Uyghur community from practising their faith and from developing economically. In an interview, she said:

> They propagate for atheism, and their main goal for 60 years was to root out Islam just because the Uyghurs are Muslims... There is a fight against Islam and Muslims and the Muslim World does not know about it. The Chinese authorities could not do that in the past, but now if Chinese soldiers see a Uyghur woman putting a headscarf on in the street, they forcefully take it off and detain her... They forced many clerics to burn the Qur'an on the streets. Because of international pressure, now you can have a copy of the Qur'an in your home, but if you have Hadeeth or other Islamic history books, or ones about the history of Prophet Muhammed, you are arrested and put in jail. What I want from the Islamic world is to put pressure on the Chinese government to allow the Uyghur youth to learn their own religion and to have religious education and to have whatever they want... I advocate for the peaceful realisation of democracy, human rights, and freedom – all fundamental

elements for a prosperous society – in East Turkestan.[3]

Rebiya Kadeer is a remarkable woman who was born into poverty and forced to leave her home. She is a loving mother to eleven children, a spiritual mother to her nation and a businesswoman who turned a one-woman laundry business into a multimillion-dollar trading empire. In 2009, she published her autobiography, *Dragon Fighter: One Woman's Epic Struggle for Peace with China*, which presents the story of her journey from humble beginnings to her position as a powerful fighter for Uyghur self-determination.

---

[3] Rashdan, Abdelrahman. "Meeting the Uyghur Leader Rebiya Kadeer." August 3, 2016.

Reflections

- Rebiya is a prominent activist who advocates for the Uyghurs. We should raise awareness about the oppression of the Uyghur people and pray for their safety and that of the whole Muslim ummah. Share articles and any news about oppressed people via social media and word of mouth.

- Rebiya's upbringing taught her the Islamic values of sacrificing for others and loving for others what we love for ourselves. We should follow her example and sacrifice our time and money towards good causes by volunteering, giving charity and sharing our food with family, neighbours, and friends if possible.

- If we are blessed enough to live in a country where we have the freedom to practise our faith, then we should use that opportunity. Most of us are extremely blessed to have the opportunity to pray, fast, wear hijab, recite the Qur'an, give dawah, seek knowledge and be openly and confidently Muslim. We need to remember the difficulties that Muslims like the Uyghurs face daily as they try to cling to their beliefs and continue to fight for their rights.

- When we see an injustice, we must remember we are not too small to speak to those in power. Rebiya met with world leaders because her cause was of the utmost importance to her. When we believe in something, we should banish self-doubt and embrace courage.

Discussion Questions
1. Who are the Uyghur people?
2. In the 21st century, why are they being persecuted and detained by the Chinese government?
3. Do the Uyghurs have any support? If so, who is helping them and how?
4. How can you spread more awareness of the Uyghur cause?
5. Rebiya was inspired by the story her father told her as a child. What story most inspires you and why?
6. Why do you feel Rebiya's story is important to share?

Hawa Aden Mohamed

An Educator and Social Activist

20th century, Somalia

Hawa Aden Mohamed, nicknamed Hooyo Hawa (Mother Hawa), was born in Somalia in 1949. Unlike most in their community, Hawa's father believed in equal education for boys and girls. Hawa and her sisters were fortunate enough to attend school with their brothers. However, this did not come easily. Hawa's father was deeply criticised and challenged by the people in the community who believed that girls did not need an education and that school was a place only for boys. He stood up for his daughters and told the critics to leave his girls alone.

This was not the only obstacle in Hawa's life. Sadly, she lost her mother in childhood. Consequently, she became responsible for her family's domestic duties at a young age. Due to her heavy workload, her schooling was often disrupted. Eventually, during her teenage years, she finally had the opportunity to attend school regularly. She valued every bit of knowledge that she gained.

Life was difficult in Somalia due to ongoing conflicts and

frequent droughts. Life was even more difficult for girls. Many girls were and still are subjected to a harmful procedure known as female genital mutilation (FGM), which is a violation of a girl's health and safety. Countless girls have lost their lives because of it and continue to suffer up until this day. FGM is a common and dangerous cultural practice that is still forced upon girls falsely in the name of Islam, when in truth, religion has nothing to do with it.

Before Hawa was born, her elder sister died at the age nine from tetanus because of FGM. Her father was against FGM but had no support and therefore was unable to prevent the procedure. Due to FGM being considered an important cultural ritual, Hawa's stepmother believed it was her responsibility to ensure this horrendous procedure was performed on Hawa and her sister. Like many of her contemporaries, her stepmother did not understand that there was no benefit in it, only harm. Hawa only learned the reason for her elder sister's death after FGM had been done to her, too. She believes that if her father had found support, she and her sister would have been saved from the experience.

Hawa went on to achieve great things in her life. She earned a teacher's diploma in Mogadishu, studied in India, and received Bachelor's and Master's degrees in child development and food science. She travelled to England, the United States and Tanzania to quench her thirst for knowledge. For over a decade, she was director of the women's education department within the Somali government.

In 1991, Hawa fled to Canada as a refugee during the civil war. In Toronto, she worked for a women's health organisation and educated immigrant Somali women about FGM. In 1994, she received Ontario's Woman of the Year Award in 1994 for her outstanding work.

Despite the risks to her safety, Hawa bravely returned to her war-torn homeland in 1995 to educate people on women's health issues. She opened an education centre in Kismayo to teach women life skills and to make them aware of their rights. Unfortunately, the school fell into the hands of the militia and was no longer safe. Hawa had to flee for safety once again.

Hawa did not lose hope in a better future for her people, despite the many setbacks that she faced. She poured blood, sweat and tears into the Galkayo Education Centre for Peace and Development (GECPD) in Puntland, Somalia in 1999. The Centre's aim was to help women and girls who had been displaced as a result of the civil war by providing free education to 120 girls. At that time, all schools were fee-based, and it was mostly boys who had the opportunity to receive an education. Eliminating school fees and providing free education to girls was a breakthrough.

At first, the school did not have any furniture, and the girls had to sit on the floor. However, with help and funding from various non-governmental organisations (or NGOs), they were able to get all the equipment they needed. Today, it is a successful educational and vocational centre.

Initially, the centre was not welcomed by the community. Hawa and her colleagues were accused of being traitors to Somali tradition. The school was so unpopular that people threw stones and vandalised the building. Despite the stone-throwing protestors, Hawa and her colleagues turned up every day and unlocked the centre's doors for the vulnerable girls who sought an education. They breathed a deep sigh of relief when the elders of the community were finally convinced that the centre was a source of good for the community and not evil as was previously thought.

The Galkayo Education Centre for Peace and Development became popular, and more girls attended with the support of the community. Now, hundreds of girls attend the school every year, and there is even a part-time programme for students who cannot attend full time. Apart from receiving a formal education and learning life skills, the girls are also taught about human rights, violence against women and peacebuilding. The school also educates them about their rights as women, the contributions they can provide for society and the dangers of FGM. Since its establishment, the GECPD has assisted more than 215,000 people.

As Hawa got older and became even more educated, she learned that FGM has no place in Islam. Desperate to protect other girls from the traumatic experiences of her own childhood, she made the decision to do everything in her power to protect the rights of girls and women. Hawa could not change the fact that her sister had died from FGM, but it became her life goal to fight for the protection of every other girl who was at risk of or had already undergone this traumatic procedure.

Among many other great accomplishments, Hawa worked hard and successfully developed an educational programme for the most vulnerable in her society. She also built a hostel and an orphanage for refugee schoolgirls to provide them with a healthy environment where they could concentrate on learning instead of worrying about food and shelter. Changing the future of girls in Somalia has been Hawa's life mission, and she has said that she will not stop until she has done her part to protect every single girl at risk.

Hawa has won various awards for her outstanding achievements in defending the rights of women and children. These include the Amnesty International Ginetta Sagan Award in 2005 for championing women's rights and the 2012 Nansen Refugee Award.

Hawa believes that with education, women and girls can break the cycle of abuse in their own lives and in their families. She spoke out when no one else did for the betterment of her community. She said: 'I think not having education is a kind of disease.. Without education, you are unaware of so many things.. Without education you do not exist much – physically yes, but mentally and emotionally, you do not exist. It's time for the culture to change. We need to keep the good and let go of the bad. And the good is to empower the girl."[4]

Hawa is a remarkable woman who, despite the hardships and countless obstacles put in her path, realised the importance of education and used it to make a positive difference in her society. She put her own life at risk by returning to the conflict-filled homeland she was forced to flee, just so she could help the most vulnerable in her community by empowering them with education and safety.

---

[4] "Somalia's Hawa Aden Mohamed Wins 2012 Nansen Refugee Award." UNHCR Press Release. September 18, 2012.

Reflections

- Our lives don't need to end the same way they started. Hawa's life was full of hardships, but she did not let her childhood experiences or the culture around her define her future.

- Hawa faced opposition and cruelty from her community, but she didn't abandon her dream of creating safety and education for girls and women. She knew that people fear what they do not understand. To change this, she kept speaking to the people in her community until they understood the importance of the centre.

- Hawa never forgot where she came from. She gave back to her community. By educating students at her school about the importance of improving their homeland, she increased the likelihood that those young people will also someday give back and help rebuild Somalia.

- Gather support. Hawa believed that if her father had the support he needed, then she and her sister would not have been subjected to FGM. When we want to make a positive change, we should try to gather as much support as possible by speaking to family, classmates, and people in the community. We can gather support by writing a blog, starting a petition, or having regular meetings with others about the things we believe in.

- Believe that it only takes one person to spark change. Hawa's father was pressured to prevent his daughters from attending school, but he stood his ground and did not cave in. Hawa's father was a true inspiration to her. Perhaps if we find the strength to stand by what we believe in, we can be the inspiration for someone else to make a positive contribution to their community.

- We should be grateful for our education, just as Hawa was. We should not take it for granted, as many children around the world do not have access to free education or the opportunity to attend school.

- Each time Hawa faced a setback, she did not give up. Instead, she started another project from scratch until she achieved success. If something really matters to us, we should keep going no matter how many obstacles come in our way.

Discussion Questions

1. What do you think is more important: what people think or what Allah ﷺ thinks of us?

2. Why was life difficult in Somalia?

3. Why is Hawa's work essential?

4. What positive change would you like to see in the world?

5. How should peer pressure be dealt with?

Anisa Rasooli

The First Female Supreme Court Judge in Afghanistan
20th century, Afghanistan

Justice Anisa Rasooli was born in 1969 in Parwan, Afghanistan. She has degrees in law and political science, a Master's degree in criminal justice, and she completed the Judicial Special Course mandated by the Supreme Court. She is a founding board member of the Afghan Women Judges' Association and a member of the International Association of Women Judges.

Anisa came from an educated family. Four of her brothers are doctors, one has a Master's degree in law, and another is an engineer. Her immediate family was supportive of her education, but her other relatives were not happy that she went to school. They did not want her to pursue her studies and go on to university. This strong disapproval was why Anisa's three elder sisters didn't have the opportunity to study. However, Anisa was fortunate, as she had the full backing of her father, her mother, and her brothers, who would not let anything stand in the way of her education.

After she graduated, Anisa's hard work and dedication paid off and she successfully became a judge in the Kabul Public

Security Court. Things changed in the 1990s when all the women judges, including Anisa, were removed from the judiciary by the Taliban when they took over Afghanistan. During this time, Anisa migrated to Pakistan, where she taught at a high school in Peshawar. After a year and a half, she returned to Parwan, a province in Afghanistan. Anisa turned her attention to teaching girls who had missed school because of the Taliban's rules. She founded a school for them, which has now become a public school, with over two thousand students.

When the interim government was established in 2001, Anisa was appointed as the Head of the Kabul Juvenile Court and then the head of the Juvenile Appellate Court. This was followed by her appointment as head of the Appellate Court's division for serious crimes of corruption. Anisa became a judicial adviser to the Afghan Supreme Court for nonviolent offenders. She also lectured and taught Afghan constitutional law, women's rights in Islam, juvenile justice, international human rights, family law, inheritance law and fair punishment.

Despite the obstacles she faced, Justice Anisa achieved success as one of the most renowned judges in Afghanistan and became a powerful advocate for women, inspiring many to pursue judicial careers. In 2018, Justice Anisa Rasooli became the first woman to occupy a seat on the Supreme Court of Afghanistan, which is the country's highest judicial position.

There are many challenges faced by female judges in Afghanistan. In some places, it is both difficult and dangerous to work as a female judge, as the very presence of women outside the house is not accepted. The brave work that Anisa does means she has to deal with extremely dangerous criminals and corrupt individuals. Her personal safety and security are constantly at risk. The work that she undertakes demands huge courage and commitment daily. However, Anisa remains faithful to the oath she took to fight for justice in Afghanistan. Justice Anisa has been the recipient of numerous letters of appreciation and medals from the Supreme Court, the Ministry of Women's Affairs, the Afghan Women Network and the Peace Jirga.

When Anisa first began her career over 23 years ago, there were only 20 female judges in Afghanistan. Afghanistan now has 300 female judges. Justice Anisa believes the presence of women in the system will encourage more women to use the judicial system to seek their rights. She believes that they will feel reassured that women judges will not turn a blind eye to violence and other crimes against women. Anisa hopes this will also encourage more women to become judges. She believes it is a woman's right to pursue what she considers a sacred profession: one in which you help others and yourself.

In the words of Justice Anisa Rasooli, 'Afghan women can be the best engineers, doctors, judges, and teachers. We are vocal and visible and playing prominent roles. We have many good things to offer if the conditions are right.'[s]

---

[s] "In the words of Justice Anisa Rasooli: "Not all women in Afghanistan are women in

REMARKABLE Muslim Women

blue burqas begging... we can be the best engineers, doctors, judges, teachers." ReliefWeb. November 7, 2018.

Reflections

- Like Justice Anisa, we too can become an inspiration for others to fulfil their dreams and to work for a just cause.

- We do not always get what we want when we want it. It comes when the time is right for us. Have patience and trust Allah's ﷻ plan.

- When one door closes, we can try to open a new door with the support of Al-Fattah ﷻ (The Opener).

- Justice Anisa's work is at times dangerous, but her greater purpose is in working for women's rights. She chose the path regardless of obstacles that come her way. Her strength is inspired from the Qur'an, where women's rights are clear, and the Qur'an's stance remains true to this day.

Discussion Questions

1. How did Judge Anisa Rasooli inspire change?

2. *It is important to read and learn about Islam from authentic sources, such as the Qur'an, hadith and reliable works, rather than believe what you see/hear/read on the media, such as news corporations or television. It's also unfair to judge Islam based on the actions of Muslims.* Would you agree with this statement?

3. Do you think people and organisations can change for the better? Does everyone deserve a second chance?

4. If something bad happens in a 'Muslim' country, is Islam to blame? Or should the person who commits the crime be solely blamed?

Sara Minkara

An Advocate for the Blind Community
20th century, United States

Sara Minkara is a Lebanese American Muslim woman. In the summer of 1996, she woke up on her seventh birthday, and her life changed forever. As she stood on the balcony of her family's summer house in Lebanon, where the enormous mountains were normally in clear view, she turned to her mother and said, 'Mum, I can't see the mountains.'

Her mother's heart sank. In that moment, she realised that her second daughter had become blind. Sara's elder sister had lost her sight on her seventh birthday two years earlier. Her mother hugged Sara tightly and reassured her that everything was going to be okay. Sara's family – especially her beloved mother – and community never allowed Sara or her sister to feel less than anyone else. They never allowed negative narratives about disability, including a lack of expectations, to ever enter their home.

Sara's parents believed that what Allah ﷺ had decreed was a blessing, and they accepted it fully. They never questioned why this happened to her and her sister. Instead, they took their strength from Islam. Their blindness was normalised in their home, and instead of feeling pitied, the girls felt empowered. They were encouraged to tap into their potential and the abilities that Allah ﷻ had given them. Sara and her parents had full faith in Allah ﷻ and knew He would never test them with things they couldn't handle. Allah ﷻ says in the Qur'an:

> *Allah does not burden a soul with more than it can handle.*
> Qur'an, Surah al-Baqarah, 2:286

Sara and her sister attended public school in America. Sara went to Wellesley College and majored in maths and economics. She then attended Harvard University's Kennedy School of Government, where she pursued a master's in public policy. Sara was enabled by her faith and by the confidence that her family had instilled in her. She wasn't afraid of adventure and lived her life to the fullest, sliding down a volcano in Nicaragua, swimming with sharks in Belize, tandem bicycling through a jungle in Bali and much more.

Sara realised that the human capacity to accomplish amazing things is greater than we think. She was grateful for the awe-inspiring experiences in her life. She knew that she and her sister were able to accomplish what they did because they were blessed to have the space and ability to explore their capacity and potential. She also knew that most people with disabilities didn't have that opportunity. When she visited Lebanon, Sara witnessed how people with disabilities were viewed negatively. Their disability was looked upon as something that should be

hidden. She understood how such negative assumptions and attitudes could affect disabled people, leading to feelings of inadequacy, disempowerment, and low self-esteem.

Sara wanted to change these negative perceptions of disability. In 2009, she won a Clinton Foundation Grant and founded a non-profit organisation called Empowerment Through Integration (ETI). ETI focuses on changing the narrative surrounding disability from a charity-based perspective to a value-based perspective. ETI work with blind children in Lebanon to instil confidence by teaching life skills, like how to walk with a white cane and how to use a computer. ETI is made up of two legal entities: the headquarters based in Boston and ETI Lebanon; it impacts thousands of individuals across Lebanon and the United States.

Sara is an established public speaker and has presented at several prestigious global summits. She has received numerous awards and fellowships for her passionate work in the social sector, including the Clinton Global Initiative Outstanding Commitment Award, the Davis Peace Project Award, the Emily Bultch Peace and Justice Award, the MIT IDEAS Award, Forbes '30 Under 30'. She was also a finalist for the Harvard President's Challenge Award.

Sara is an internationally recognised advocate in disability inclusion, female leadership, and social entrepreneurship. Sara wisely said: 'Everyone needs to look at a person with a disability and see Allah has created that person and that person has a value

REMARKABLE *Muslim Women*

to give to this world and that's our mission.'[6] She would not change her blindness for the world. She believes that it has given her strength and resilience and a greater connection to Allah ﷻ. Sara is a brilliant and tenacious Muslim woman, with a wide set of talents and strong faith. She is a true visionary and a great example of excellence for us all.

---

[6] Minkara, Sara. "Enabled by Faith: Sara Minkara | Confident Muslim." Yaqeen Institute. Speech at 2018 MAS-ICNA. January 11, 2019. YouTube, 41:48.

Reflections
- Like Sara, we should accept ourselves fully. When things happen to us that we do not understand or cannot control, we should put our trust in Allah ﷻ and accept that it's Allah's ﷻ will.

- We should use our talents and skills to fulfil our full potential and focus on what we can do, and not on what we think we cannot.

- We should be mindful of how we judge and treat people. We should be wary of how our judgements can put limitations on people's abilities to reach their full potential.

- Let us thank Allah ﷻ for the blessings we have as they can be taken away at any point.

- Sometimes, what seems like a loss is an even greater blessing in disguise.

- No matter what happens in life and the difficulties we may face, we should never lose hope or give up on ourselves. It's okay to feel sad, but we should draw hope from our faith.

- Every human being deserves to be respected and welcomed. Sacred places should be made accessible to people with disabilities and we should make more of an effort to include everyone in our gatherings.

- We should aim to bring the most benefit and inspiration to those who are closest to us, as sometimes they are the ones who need us the most. Healthy and content individuals in our families will contribute, God willing, to a more fruitful and empowered society.

Discussion Questions

1. How can faith in Allah ﷻ affect a person who is experiencing hardship?
2. Why is Sara's organisation important?
3. Has Sara's story made you reflect on any negative assumptions you may have made in the past?
4. How does Sara's story inspire you?
5. Why is it so important to have a strong support system around you?
6. Can you think of something that you were first upset about, but later discovered it was a blessing?

Arfa Karim

A Genius and Computer Scientist
20th century, Pakistan

Arfa Karim Randhawa was a computer prodigy born in Faisalabad, Pakistan in 1995. Her father, Amjad Abdul Karim Randhawa, was a lieutenant colonel working for the Pakistani army; her mother, Samina Amjad, was a loving mother and homemaker. Arfa had two younger brothers. When she was six years old, she saw a computer for the first time, and it was love at first sight! She asked her father to buy her a computer of her very own. Her mind began buzzing with excitement, and she was overwhelmed with questions, eager to find out what the computer did and how exactly it worked.

Amjad made his darling daughter's heart happy by gifting her a computer. Arfa was fascinated by it and keen to use it as soon as she could. By playing with her computer and feeding her curiosity, Arfa quickly learned how to operate it. Within two years, she was able to fully operate Windows and different computer software. She would make wonderful presentations for her parents with her new computer. Arfa's parents took a keen interest in their daughter's newfound talent. Her competence on the computer baffled her parents at first, but they soon realised that their daughter had a special gift. They supported her passion and enrolled her in an IT training institute near their house.

Arfa's extraordinary skills advanced rapidly. The management of the institute were so impressed by the young girl's proficiency that they recommended that she seek Microsoft certification. She studied for her certification examinations during her four-month summer break from school. In 2004, at the age of nine, Arfa passed the Microsoft certification exam with flying colours, becoming the youngest ever Microsoft Certified Professional in the world – a title she kept until 2008. This was a ground-breaking moment for not only Arfa and her family, but for the Microsoft team and the whole country of Pakistan.

Arfa's rare and astonishing achievement caught the attention of the renowned co-founder of Microsoft himself, Bill Gates. Arfa and her family accepted Gates's invitation to visit the Microsoft headquarters in Redmond, Washington. Gates was impressed by Arfa's charming character, intelligence, and boldness. Arfa presented Gates with a handwritten poem she had composed, and, in return, he wrote a note for her with his photograph and autograph.

On her return to Pakistan, Arfa was hailed as a national treasure and received many awards. She was one of the youngest recipients of the President's Award for Pride of Performance.

In August 2005, she received the Fatimah Jinnah Gold Medal in the field of Science and Technology and the Salaam Pakistan Youth Award from the then-Prime Minister of Pakistan, Shaukat Aziz.

Arfa was interviewed by various TV channels and represented Pakistan on numerous international forums. IT professionals in Dubai invited her for a two-week stay. A dinner reception was hosted in her honour and was attended by dignitaries of Dubai and the ambassador of Pakistan. On this trip, Arfa was given various medals and awards. She also flew a plane in a Dubai flying club and received her first flight certificate at the age of ten.

In November 2006, Arfa was invited by Microsoft to be a keynote speaker at the Tech-Ed Developers Conference in Barcelona. She was the only Pakistani among over five thousand developers there. She was reportedly working on a project with NASA when something unexpected happened.

In December 2011, whilst studying at Lahore Grammar School, in her second year of A levels, Arfa suffered from cardiac arrest after an epileptic seizure. She was admitted to Lahore's Combined Military Hospital in critical condition.

Arfa, a loving daughter, sister, and computer prodigy passed away on 14 January 2012 at the age of sixteen.

Despite her extraordinary achievements at such a young age, she was a humble girl who was passionate about helping others. The nation of Pakistan mourned her death, and

REMARKABLE *Muslim Women*

in her honour, the government built a science and technology park in Lahore in her name. Also, in tribute to her, Arfa's family's village's name has been changed to Arfa Karim Nagar.

Arfa intended to support the development of her community and wanted to use her skills to help the young and underserved have access to information technology. In 2012, Arfa's parents established the Arfa Karim Foundation, a non-profit foundation that serves communities by providing support to key players in three core areas: education, social innovation, and community development. May this be accepted as a *sadaqa jariya* for Arfa and may Allah ﷻ reward Arfa for her good intentions and grant her a beautiful place in Paradise. Ameen.

Reflections

- Arfa had everything going for her and achieved more in a few years than many people do in their lifetime. She wasn't afraid to try new things. She learned about computers just by exploring one! This goes to show that we don't need to be an expert at something to learn about it, and we shouldn't be afraid of trying and exploring new things.

- Arfa's parents bought her a computer and took an interest in their daughter's passion and supported her every step of the way. When our family members, friends, or people we know become interested in something, we should support them. We don't know where it could take them.

- At times we may not receive the support of friends or family, but we should remember the people that have no one have Allah and His help and support is sufficient for us. Instead of feeling disheartened, we should speak to Allah about our goals and remember that our success is only by Allah. *My success lies only with God. In Him I trust, and to Him I turn.* Qur'an Surah Hud, 11:88

- Arfa had many good intentions before she passed away. As Muslims, we are rewarded for our good intentions, so we should try to make as many good intentions as possible. Like Arfa, we should do our best and leave the rest to Allah ﷻ.

- A long life isn't guaranteed to anyone. We should do as much good as possible and always remember to make dua for protection and ask Allah ﷻ to accept and bless the good work that we do.

Discussion Questions

1. Do you think some people fear failure? Could this hold them back from trying new things?

2. What difference does it make when a person pursuing their goals is supported by their friends and family?

3. If people don't get the support they want, should they give up on their dreams?

Razan al-Najjar

A Palestinian Medic and Hero
20th century, Palestine

Razan al-Najjar was born in Gaza, Palestine in September 1997. She was the eldest of six children. Her father, Ashraf al-Najjar, previously worked in Israel in the scrap metal business until travel across the border was prohibited. He then worked in the Gaza Strip as a motorbike mechanic before becoming unemployed.

Razan's short life was filled with tragedy. She lived through three devastating wars: the Gaza Massacre (December 2008–January 2009), Operation Pillar of Defence (14–21 November 2012) and the 2014 Israel-Gaza conflict, in which her neighbourhood was destroyed.

The history of Palestine is filled with tragedy. In 1948, Israel forced nearly a million Palestinians from their homes and did not let them return. Since then, Palestinians have been persecuted, killed, and systemically oppressed by Israeli occupation. The Great March of Return, launched on 30 March 2018, is an ongoing campaign with protests each Friday in the Gaza Strip near the Gaza-Israel border. Protestors demand that Palestinian refugees and their descendants be allowed to return to the land they were displaced from (now considered Israeli territory) and that the blockade of the Gaza Strip be terminated.

Thanks to the Israeli occupation's horrific impact on the Gazan economy, Razan could not afford a university education. However, this did not stop her from learning and making a positive contribution to her community. She sought out free educational opportunities and studied both calligraphy and nursing. Razan trained as a paramedic in Khan Younis at Nasser Hospital and became an active member of the Palestinian Medical Relief Society, a non-governmental health organisation. As she witnessed the enormous suffering of her people, Razan took it upon herself to do something constructive. She began by helping those injured by Israeli soldiers during the Great March of Return protests.

Razan was the first woman to volunteer as a medic and to go to the border when the protests began, and she soon became an icon in the Gaza Strip. Local media published many images of her online, including photos of her nursing the injured with her white coat splashed with the blood of her patients.

In an interview with Al Jazeera media, she shared that an Israeli soldier had shot directly at her several times as a warning not to tend to the wounded in the protests. Razan and her fellow Gazan medics followed a strategy to avoid being shot by Israeli snipers. They wore white coats and moved slowly and deliberately towards casualties with their hands raised above

Razan al-Najjar

their heads. They passed piles of burning tyres and plumes of white tear gas smoke as they approached the fence. When within speaking distance of the troops on the other side, they shouted out in unison, 'Don't shoot. There are wounded.'

Razan was tending to those injured during protests at the fence during Ramadan on 1 June 2018. The brave medic took all of her usual precautions by wearing her uniform – a white jacket with reflective, high visibility stripes – and by following protocol when going to help a distressed protestor who was calling for help. However, on that Friday, she was struck in the chest by a bullet from Israeli forces and mercilessly killed at the tender age of twenty-one. On that same day, more than one hundred Palestinians were injured, forty of whom were shot by Israeli live fire.

Razan's death sparked outrage and gripped the world's attention. Thousands of Gazans, including hundreds of medical personnel, attended Razan's funeral and mourned her death. Razan's mother, Um Ahmed al-Najjar, and her sister, Rayan al-Najjar, have continued Razan's legacy of saving the lives of unarmed Palestinian people who are attacked by Israeli forces. Like Razan, these brave women stand strong in the face of danger. In Um Ahmed's words, 'All Palestinian people are Razan, and all Arab and Muslim countries are Razan.'[7]

---

[7] "The family of the slain Palestinian medic Razan al Najjar has a message for you." TRT World. June 9, 2018. YouTube video.

Razan once said in an interview, 'I hope that I can be a role model for every girl that sees me. And every girl that wants to be like me, God willing, will be like me and better than me. I will continue, and I will face all the difficulties, despite incurring many injuries – but praise be to God I will continue my journey to return [to pre-1948 Palestine] by the permission of God.'[8]

Razan was a remarkable woman who risked her life to help her people. She lived and died for what she believed in. Her short life had major impact and substantial value. She was fierce, outspoken, and deeply loved by those who knew her.

---

[8] "Who Was Razan al Najjar, the Palestinian Paramedic Israel killed?" Middle East Eye. March 30, 2019.

Reflections

- The bravery that Razan displayed and the risk she took in helping defenceless Palestinian protestors demonstrates the beauty of her character and strength.

- The occupiers may take away their land, but they'll never take their resilience and *iman*.

- Although she was poor and could not afford a university education, Razan did not become hopeless. Instead, she searched for opportunities and then used these to benefit her people and help the wounded.

- Razan's life was short but full of purpose. We should reflect on this and find ways to maximise the opportunities that we have to benefit those in need.

- Razan did not despair because of the great tragedy of her people and their oppression by the Israeli army. On the contrary, she derived strength and motivation from her people's steadfastness despite the obstacles they faced.

- Even though she became a local celebrity, Razan's goal was, 'to save lives and evacuate (wounded) people. We do this for our country.'[9] Make your purpose your goal and you will, God willing, be content.

Discussion Questions

1. In the media there is a difference when it comes to reporting Palestine, compared to other countries where war is taking place. Why do you think that is?

2. Why is it important to raise awareness and assist the Palestinian cause?

3. What made Razan the hero she was?

---

[9] Alsaafin, Lina and Maram Humaid. "In Gaza, Grief and Pain for Slain 'Angel of Mercy' Paramedic." Al Jazeera. June 2, 2018.

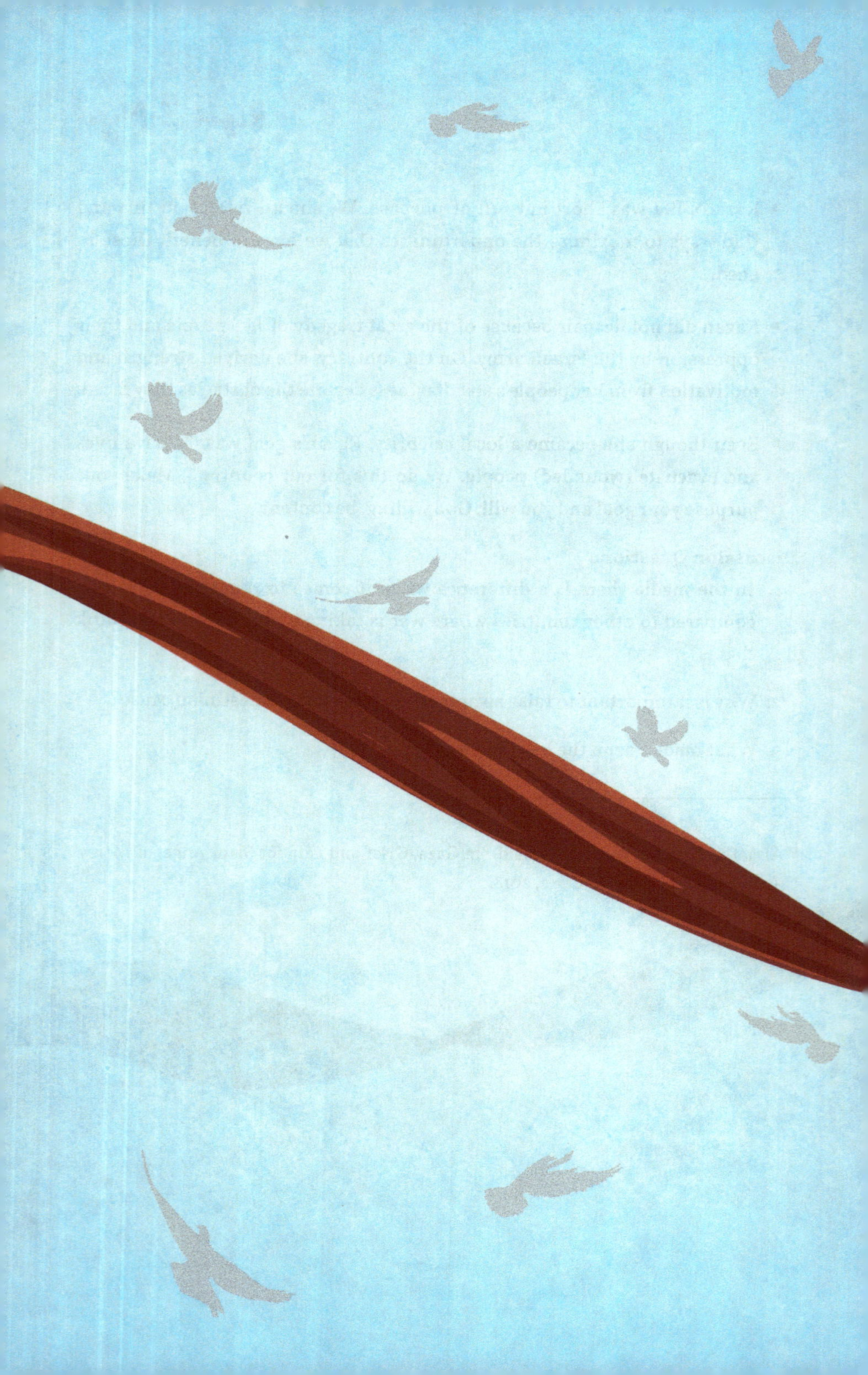

Acknowledgements

First and foremost, I would like to thank and praise Allah ﷻ for allowing me to write this book. It has been truly an honour to delve into the lives of all the remarkable women mentioned in this book and share them with my readers, alhamdulillah. I would like to thank my husband and my children for their patience, prayers, and support. I would like to say a special thanks (jazakallah khair) to Shaykh Dr Saalim Al-Azhari for his generosity in answering my questions and for his time and effort. I would like to thank my parents for their love and prayers, Anhha Chowdhury for being my biggest supporter and a true blessing in my life, my beta readers and my editors Laura El Alam, Jessica Hassan, and Zainab bint Younus for being a pleasure to work with, Sheeba Shaikh for creating a phenomenal cover and book design and Dr Nafeesa Qureshi for her time. May Allah ﷻ reward you all immensely and bless and accept this work from us. Ameen.

Glossary

administration: the management of public affairs, government

admonition: a firm warning or reprimand

ancestry: one's family or ethnic descent

angler: a person who fishes with a rod and line

Ansar: 'the helpers', the local inhabitants of Madinah who took the Prophet Muhammad ﷺ and his followers into their homes when they emigrated from Makkah

appellate: of or relating to appeals (where people who have been convicted of a crime can appeal against their conviction)

aristocrat: a person of high social rank, who belongs to the aristocracy

buoy: to prevent someone or something from sinking, to sustain or encourage, to float or rise by reason of lightness

caliph: the chief Muslim civil and religious ruler in an Islamic state or government

caliphate: the geographical land and peoples that fall under the governance of a caliph (like a kingdom)

civil war: a war between citizens of the same country

colonial: relating to or characteristic of a colony or colonies

colony: a country or area under the full or partial political control of another country and occupied by settlers from that country

commodity: any useful or valuable thing, especially something that is bought and sold. Grain, coffee and precious metals are all commodities.

conspiracy: a secret plan by a group to do something unlawful or harmful

convert: to change to a different religion, belief, or opinion

curtail: to reduce in extent or quantity; impose a restriction on

da'iya: a caller to Islam

dawah: an Arabic word which means to invite, call or summon someone. This term is often used to describe when Muslims teach others about Islam

dirham: a currency used in the Middle East

displace: to expel or force to flee from home or homeland

dissident: a person who opposes official policy, especially that of an authoritarian state

drought: a prolonged period of abnormally low rainfall, leading to a shortage of water

earl: (the title of) a British man of high social rank

elegy: a poem of serious reflection, typically a lament for the dead

entrepreneur: a person who sets up a business or businesses, taking on financial risks in the hope of profit

estuary: the tidal mouth of a large river, where the tide meets the stream

exile: the state of being barred from one's native country, typically for political or punitive reasons

expedition: a journey undertaken by a group of people with a particular purpose, especially that of exploration, research, or war

female genital mutilation (FGM): the practice, traditional in some cultures, of partially or totally removing the external genitalia of girls and young women for non-medical reasons

forefather: a member of the past generations of one's family or people, an ancestor

governance: the action or manner of governing a state, organisation, etc.

governess: (especially in the past) a woman who lives with a family and teaches their children at home

guerrilla warfare: a kind of war where people not in an army use army tactics to fight against another group

hadith: sayings and actions of the Prophet ﷺ

hafidha: a girl or woman who has memorised the Qur'an

hajj: the pilgrimage to Makkah, which all Muslims are expected to make at least once during their lifetime if they can afford to do so. It is one of the five pillars of Islam.

Hejaz: a coastal region of the western Arabian Peninsula bordering on the Red Sea, including both Makkah and Madinah. It was formerly an independent kingdom until it united with Najd to form the Kingdom of Saudi Arabia.

Iberian: relating to Iberia, or the countries of Spain and Portugal

imam: a person who leads prayers in a masjid

innovative: using new methods or ideas

inscribe: to write words in a book or carve them into an object

interim government: a provisional government

Jahiliyya: 'the age of ignorance', a term used in reference to the time prior to the advent of Islam

jaji: a teacher leader of the Yan Taru movement

Jannah: Paradise

jurisprudence: the theory or philosophy of law, a legal system

juvenile: a young person

lament: a passionate expression of grief, often in music, poetry or song form

Makkans: the people of Makkah

malfa: a hat which was a traditional symbol of office tied with a red turban

martyr: (1) a person who willingly suffers death rather than renounce his or her religion; (2) a person who is put to death or endures great suffering on behalf of any belief, principle or cause masjid

Mayfair: a fashionable and wealthy district in the West End of London

mediation: intervention in a dispute in order to resolve it

military: relating to or characteristic of soldiers or armed forces

militia: (1) a military force that is raised from the civil population to supplement a regular army in an emergency; (2) a military force that engages in rebel or terrorist activities in opposition to a regular army

monarch: a sovereign head of state, especially a king, queen or emperor

monotheism: the belief that there is only one God

monotheistic: relating to or characterised by the belief that there is only one God

moor: an open area of hills covered with rough grass, especially in Britain

Muslimah: a Muslim woman

narcissistic: having or showing an excessive interest in or admiration of oneself and one's physical appearance

navy: the branch of the armed services of a state that conducts military operations at sea

non-governmental organisation (NGO): a non-profit organisation that operates independently of any government, typically one whose purpose is to address a social or political issue

peer: in the UK, a person who has a high social position and any of a range of titles, such as baron, earl and duke

pilgrimage: religious journey

pioneer: one of the first people to do something important that is later continued and developed by other people

prestigious: respected and admired, usually because of being important

privateer: an armed ship owned and crewed by private individuals

individuals holding a government commission and authorised for use in war, especially in the capture of merchant shipping

proficiency: a high degree of skill; expertise

prolific: present in large numbers or quantities; plentiful

Reconquista: a long series of wars and battles between the Christian Kingdoms and the Muslims for control of the Iberian Peninsula. It lasted for a good portion of the Middle Ages from 718 to 1492.

refugee: a person who has been forced to leave their country in order to escape war, persecution or natural disaster

remarkable: unusual or special and therefore surprising and worth mentioning

renowned: known or talked about by many people; famous

resistance: the refusal to accept or comply with something

ritual: a religious or solemn ceremony consisting of a series of actions performed according to a prescribed order

sahaabiyaat: the female companions of the Prophet ﷺ

salaam: peace

salawat: prayer or salutation

secular: not connected with religious or spiritual matters

secularism: a belief that rejects religion, or the belief that religion should not be a part of the affairs of the public life

self-determination: (1) the free choice of one's own acts or states without external compulsion; (2) determination by the people of a territorial unit of their own future political status

shahadah: the testimony of faith

statesmanship: skill in managing public affairs

stereotype: a widely held and oversimplified image or idea of a particular type of person or thing

stigmatise: to treat someone or something unfairly by disapproving of him or her

sultan: a Muslim sovereign

Sunnah: the way of the Prophet ﷺ in words and actions

Supreme Court: the highest judicial court in a country or state

tafsir: the explanation of the meanings of the Qur'an

Taliban: ultraconservative political and religious faction that emerged in Afghanistan in the mid-1990s and took control

tenacious: a tenacious person is determined and is not willing to stop when they are trying to achieve something

tetanus: a bacterial disease marked by rigidity and spasms of the voluntary muscles

theology: the study of the nature of God and religious belief

trading: the action or activity of buying and selling goods and services

triumphant: victorious, successful

tyrant: a cruel and oppressive ruler

Umm al-Mu'minin: a mother of the believers, a blessed title given to the wives of the Prophet ﷺ

umrah: the optional lesser pilgrimage made by Muslims to Makkah, which may be performed at any time of the year

UNESCO: the acronym for the United Nations Educational, Scientific and Cultural Organisation

Uyghur: (1) a member of a Turkic people powerful in Mongolia and East Turkestan between the eighth and twelfth centuries CE who constitute a majority of the population of Chinese Turkestan; (2) the Turkic language of the Uyghurs

violation: the action of violating someone or something

vizier: a high official in some Muslim countries

warfare: engagement in or the activities involved in war or conflict

wet nurse: a woman employed to suckle another woman's child

Yan Taru: Nana Asma'u's educational movement, meaning 'those who congregate together'

Bibliography

HAAJAR

Suleiman, Omar. "The Story of Hajar: Uncovering Certainty in Uncertainty." Yaqeen Institute. August 14, 2019. https://yaqeeninstitute.org/omar-suleiman/the-story-of-hajar-uncovering-certainty-in-uncertainty-sh-omar-suleiman-lecture.

AASIYA BINT MUZAHIM

Ibn Kathir. *Stories of the Prophets*. Beirut: Dar al-Kutub al-Ilmiyah, 1987.

Suleiman, Omar. "The Pious Wife of a Tyrant (Asiya bint Muzahim) - Women of Paradise." Qur'an Weekly. March 12, 2014. YouTube video, 14:46. https://www.youtube.com/watch?v=f0gkYZpYstc.

KHADIJAH BINT KHUWAYLID

Qadhi, Yasir. "Khadijah - The Mother of the Believers." Yasir Qadhi. September 18, 2012. YouTube video, 1:23:43. https://www.youtube.com/watch?v=1_H95i_go5M.

Qutb, Muhammad. *Women Around the Messenger*. N.p.: International Islamic Publishing House (2007).

AISHA BINT ABU BAKR

Suleiman, Omar. "Our Mother, Our Teacher (Aisha bint Abu-Bakr) - Women of Paradise." Qur'an Weekly. March 19, 2014. YouTube video, 14:00. https://www.youtube.com/watch?v=flgYPlycrVs.

RUFAIDA AL-ASLAMIYYAH

"She was the FIRST Muslim Nurse | The Muslim Lady." One Path Network. February 5, 2020. YouTube video, 2:26. https://www.youtube.com/watch?v=rA36cIlB7Lo.

Abdul Saputra, Ading Kusdiana, and Tolib Rahmatillah. "Rufaidah Al-Aslamiyah: Perawat Pertama di Dunia Islam (Abad 6-7 M.)."

Historia Madania: Jurnal Ilmu Sejarah, July 2020. https://www.researchgate.net/publication/345280900_Rufaidah_AlAslamiyah_Perawat_Pertama_di_Dunia_Islam_Abad_6-7_M.

NUSAYBA BINT KA'AB

Kahlawi, Abla. "The Best Women on Earth - Ep 27 - Um Amarah Al Ansari." Qanat Iqra' al-Fadaa'iyyah. December 24, 2013. YouTube video, 21:20. https://www.youtube.com/watch?v=L6DIR0YHJ-8.

Ghadanfar, Mahmood Ahmad. *Great Women of Islam: Who Were Given the Good News of Paradise*. Riyadh: Darussalam, 2001

FATIMA AL-FIHRI

Carrington, Daisy. "Al-Qarawiyyin – World's Oldest Library – Gets Facelift in Fez, Morocco." CNN. March 2, 2017. https://edition.cnn.com/travel/article/worlds-oldest-library-al-qarawiyyin/index.html.

"Medina of Fez." UNESCO. https://whc.unesco.org/en/list/170/.

"Muslims that Changed the World: Fatimah Al-Fihri." Ministryofdawah07. June 21, 2011. YouTube video, 38:42. https://www.youtube.com/watch?v=FaLU8Ul5uHY&t=0s.

"See the World's Most Beautiful Libraries." *National Geographic*. January 5, 2019. https://www.nationalgeographic.co.uk/photography/2019/01/see-worlds-most-beautiful-libraries?image=al-qarawiyyin-mosque-university-fes-morocco.

"The Firsts - Fatimah al-Fihri." Muslimah Media. February 4, 2015. YouTube video, 5:10. https://www.youtube.com/watch?v=zENLxANuGas.

Errazzouki, Samia. Images of Fatima and Maryam al-Firi's diplomas. April 1, 2022. Twitter. https://twitter.com/S_Errazzouki/status/1510129277735366667?t=097JEcPjjAdgRCd_n7Uuuw&s=08

RAZIYA SULTAN

"Talking History |3| Razia Sultana - the Sultan of Dilli." Rajya Sabha TV. June 21, 2017. YouTube video, 23:47. https://www.youtube.com/watch?v=JyNs_KvzpQU.

Verde, Tom. "Malika II: Radiyya bint Iltutmish." AramcoWorld. May/June 2016.

SAYYIDA AL-HURRA

Birjas, Yasir. "The Odyssey of a Forgotten Nation, The Moriscos of Spain (Pt 1)." Muslim Matters. October 26, 2009. https://muslimmatters.org/2009/10/26/the-odyssey-of-a-forgotten-nation-the-moriscos-of-spain-pt-1/.

"Medina of Tétouan (formerly known as Titawin)." UNESCO. https://whc.unesco.org/en/list/837/.

Sánchez, Juan Pablo. "This 16th-Century Corsair Was the Most Feared Pirate of the Mediterranean." *National Geographic*. October 12, 2019. https://www.nationalgeographic.co.uk/history-and-civilisation/2019/10/16th-century-corsair-was-most-feared-pirate-mediterranean.

Verde, Tom. "Malika VI: Sayyida Al-Hurra." Aramco World. January/February 2017.

Wikipedia, s.v. "Forced Conversions of Muslims in Spain." Last updated February 12, 2021, 18:43. https://en.wikipedia.org/wiki/Forced_conversions_of_Muslims_in_Spain.

NANA ASMA'U

Cartwright, Mark. "Hausaland." May 9, 2019. https://www.worldhistory.org/Hausaland/.

Murad, Abdal Hakim Murad. "Nana Asma'u – Paradigms of Leadership." Cambridge Muslim College. January 12, 2019. https://www.youtube.com/watch?v=3bAMRxWgCNo.

"Nana Asma'u and the 'Yan Taru Movement.'" Daily Trust. June 3, 2017.

https://dailytrust.com/nana-asmau-and-the-yan-taru-movement.

CUT NYAK DHIEN

Ohorella, Benny and Zaynab El-Fatah. "Tjoet Njak Dien." Victory News Magazine. 1999. http://www.victorynewsmagazine.com/TjoetNjakDien.htm.

"Tjut Nyak Dien." Women's Islamic Initiative in Spirituality and Equality. http://www.wisemuslimwomen.org/muslim-woman/tjut-njak-dien-10/.

LADY EVELYN COBBOLD

Cobbold, Lady Evelyn. *Pilgrimage to Mecca*. London: Arabian Publishing, 1934.

ŞULE YÜKSEL ŞENLER

Saleem, Hamza. "Imprisoned for Hijab: The Story of Şule Yüksel Şenler." Islam21C.com. September 3, 2019.

"Schools Ordered Shut in India as Hijab Ban Protests Intensify." Al Jazeera. February 8, 2022. https://www.aljazeera.com/amp/news/2022/2/8/schools-ordered-shut-in-india-as-hijab-ban-protests-intensify.

"Şule Yüksel Şenler: Icon for Muslim Women Passes Away." *Daily Sabah*. August 29, 2019.

ZAINAB AL-GHAZALI

"Hajja Zaynab Al-Ghazzali (Return of the Pharaoh)." Ilm Film. November 28, 2015. YouTube video, 28:01. https://www.youtube.com/watch?v=648W2oQ6HS0.

"Zainab Al-Ghazali." Women's Islamic Initiative in Spirituality and Equality. https://www.wisemuslimwomen.org/muslim-woman/zainab-al-ghazali-4/.

Begg, Moazzam. "The Tortured Scholar | Zaynab al-Ghazali." Islam21C. January 27, 2021. https://www.islam21c.com/islamic-thought/history/the-tortured-scholar-zaynab-al-ghazali/

REBIYA KADEER

Kadeer, Rebiya. "Rebiya Kadeer - One on One." Al Jazeera English. Interview with Riz Khan. October 10, 2010. https://www.youtube.com/watch?v=noJtQTb-YxE.

Rashdan, Abdelrahman. "Meeting the Uyghur Leader Rebiya Kadeer." August 3, 2016. https://www.academia.edu/22984954/Meeting_the_Uyghur_Leader_Rebiya_Kadeer

HAWA ADEN MOHAMED

"Hawa Aden 01." GECPD Galkacyo. October 8, 2012. YouTube video, 4:13. https://www.youtube.com/watch?v=pZtmlmrInZU.

Keung, Nicholas. "Former Toronto refugee honoured with 2012 UNHCR Nansen Refugee Award." Toronto Star. September 18, 2012. https://www.thestar.com/news/gta/2012/09/18/former_toronto_refugee_honoured_with_2012_unhcr_nansen_refugee_award.html.

Reardon, Divers. "Somali Humanitarian 'Mama' Hawa Wins 2012 Nansen Refugee Award." UNHCR/UK. September 18, 2012.

"Somalia: Giving Girls a Chance." ReliefWeb. May 30, 2007. https://reliefweb.int/report/somalia/somalia-giving-girls-chance.

"Somalia's Hawa Aden Mohamed Wins 2012 Nansen Refugee Award." UNHCR Press Release. September 18, 2012. https://www.unhcr.org/uk/news/press/2012/9/50583fdc6/somalias-hawa-aden-mohamed-wins-2012-nansen-refugee-award.html?query=Aden.

Younas, Salman. "Female Genital Mutilation." SeekersGuidance. May 4, 2019. https://seekersguidance.org/answers/hanafi-fiqh/female-genital-mutilation/.

ANISA RASOOLI

"Anisa Rasooli." International Association of Women Judges. https://www.iawj2021auckland.com/program/speakers/anisa-rasooli.html.

De Lauri, Antonio. "Women Judges in Afghanistan: An Interview with Anisa Rasooli." Chr. Michelsen Institute. 2020. https://www.cmi.no/publications/7268-women-judges-in-afghanistan-an-interview-with-anisa-rasooli.

"In the words of Justice Anisa Rasooli: "Not all women in Afghanistan are women in blue burqas begging…we can be the best engineers, doctors, judges, teachers." ReliefWeb. November 7, 2018. https://reliefweb.int/report/afghanistan/words-justice-anisa-rasooli-not-all-women-afghanistan-are-women-blue-burqas.

"Macron: Freedom for Afghan Women but Not for French Muslim Women." TRT World. August 19, 2021. https://www.trtworld.com/magazine/macron-freedom-for-afghan-women-but-not-for-french-muslim-women-49317.

SARA MINKARA

"History." Empowerment Through Integration. https://www.etivision.org/history.

Minkara, Sara. "Enabled by Faith: Sara Minkara | Confident Muslim." Yaqeen Institute. Speech at 2018 MAS-ICNA. January 11, 2019. YouTube, 41:48. https://www.youtube.com/watch?v=iWNa4ZJKz2g&feature=youtu.be.

ARFA KARIM

Abbas, Nosheen. "Arfa Randhawa Death: Pakistan Mourns IT Girl Genius." BBC. January 18, 2012. https://www.bbc.co.uk/news/world-asia-16599781.

Iqbal, Abdullah. "Faisalabad Girl Chats with Bill Gates." Gulf News. July 18, 2005.

RAZAN AL-NAJJAR

Alsaafin, Lina and Maram Humaid. "In Gaza, Grief and Pain for Slain 'Angel of Mercy' Paramedic." Al Jazeera. June 2, 2018.

Gadzo, Mersiha and Anas Jnena. "The Palestinian Women at the Forefront of Gaza's Protests." Al Jazeera. April 20, 2018.

Holmes, Oliver and Hazem Balousha. "Mother of Shot Gaza Medic: 'She Thought the White Coat Would Protect Her.'" The Guardian. June 8, 2018.

"Who Was Razan al Najjar, the Palestinian Paramedic Israel killed?" Middle East Eye. March 30, 2019. YouTube video, 2:16. https://www.youtube.com/watch?v=G2fcTIltMlY&feature=youtu.be.

"The family of the slain Palestinian medic Razan al Najjar has a message for you." TRT World. June 9, 2018. YouTube video. https://www.youtube.com/watch?v=eAUT6TS7R5Y

About the Author

Maryam Yousaf is a Scottish-Pakistani author whose goal is to change the world one book at a time. She writes to inspire children from diverse backgrounds to believe in themselves, dream big and strive to be their very best. She believes children should be reflected in the books they read in terms of their faith, race and abilities, which is why she is intentional about representing as many people as possible. She strives to portray a true representation of the richness of the Muslim faith by promoting peace and unity and addressing Islamophobia through storytelling.

She is a blogger on Instagram, by the name of @MuslimaToday and is passionate about making a positive difference to her community online as well as offline through her mobile library service and book club.

Maryam is a wife and mother to four brave hearts who inspire her every day. She enjoys going for morning walks by the beach, baking with her children and finding beauty in the simple things in life.

Other children's books by Maryam Yousaf include '*Mr Blue in Rainbow Planet*' and '*Huda's Hijab*'.

Reviews are important to help books get discovered and reach more readers.

If you enjoyed *Remarkable Muslim Women Throughout the Ages*, then please leave a review on Amazon by scanning the barcode below.

SCAN ME

The Prophet ﷺ said, 'One who guides to something good has a reward similar to that of its doer'.
(*Sahih Muslim*, no. 1893).

Spread the word and encourage others to read these remarkable stories.

To find out more about the author Maryam Yousaf and her books and to arrange author visits and events please visit our website www.muslimatoday.com where you will find free activities and details of forthcoming events, and to be the first to hear about latest releases and special offers, sign up for our newsletters.

www.ingramcontent.com/pod-product-compliance
Lightning Source LLC
Chambersburg PA
CBHW071116160426
43196CB00013B/2589